HOLLIS͞   airsen-
tient me   t.com,
the pop   edium
John Ed   FM's
Angels i   fifteen
years, H   into
everyday   public
appearances and workshops in the United States and abroad.
For more information about her work, please visit Hollister
Rand.com.

ABOUT THE AUTHOR

WALTER RAND is a clairvoyant, clairaudient, and clairsentient medium, and a regular contributor to InfiniteQuest, the popular website launched by the celebrity psychic medium John Edward. She was formerly a regular guest on KOST 103.5's Morning Waking and KBIG FM's Radio Medium. For over thirty years, Hollister's dedication to integrating mediumship into her everyday life has included private and group sessions and workshops.

I'm Not
Dead,
I'm
DIFFERENT

HARPER

NEW YORK . LONDON . TORONTO . SYDNEY

I'm Not
Dead,
I'm
DIFFERENT

Kids in Spirit

Teach Us About

Living a Better

Life on Earth

HOLLISTER RAND

HARPER

HarperCollins books may be purchased for educational, business, or sales promotional use. For information please write: Special Markets Department, HarperCollins Publishers, 10 East 53rd Street, New York, NY 10022.

FIRST EDITION

Designed by Betty Lew

Library of Congress Cataloging-in-Publication Data is available upon request.

ISBN 978-0-06-195906-6

11 12 13 14 15   OV/RRD   10 9 8 7 6 5 4 3 2 1

Dedicated to my mother,

Joan Harriet Farrer Gierisch,

whose interest in the welfare of others
became my desire to bring healing,
whose love for books inspired my writing,
and whose passion for learning taught me
to explore life . . . fearlessly.

CONTENTS

INTRODUCTION

"Wake up!" I heard a voice shout.

So I did.

It was four o'clock in the morning, still dark, and I was alone. At least, I *thought* I was alone. But I wasn't. There was a young man standing at the foot of my bed, a young man in spirit. He was fuzzy from the waist down, but there was a clear urgency in his eyes. I was startled, but not scared. This wasn't the first time that a spirit had stood at the foot of my bed. Somehow, though, I sensed that this was different. "Wake up!" he shouted again. I felt like shouting back, "You already woke me up!" but by then he was gone. Spirits like to get in the last word and this young spirit's message, though brief, was important for me to hear.

Since that early morning visit, I've come to understand that his call to "wake up" was more than just a summons to get out of bed. It was nothing short of a demand to be present, to live fully, to become aware of life in all its exuberance—to love despite the pain that comes with the separation we call death.

It's oddly ironic that I woke up to life because of a dead person. That encounter happened roughly twenty years ago. I've

learned a lot from the spirits since then, including how to listen to them during the daytime so that they don't announce
themselves at night. More important, though, I've been guided,
directed, and outright pushed by those in spirit to give them a
voice in this world.

As the above example demonstrates, there is a particularly
vocal and insistent group living on the other side—the young.
For years, other mediums had noticed the entourage of kids and
young adults that surrounded me. This struck us all as strange
because I have no children of my own, in the physical sense
anyway. Not having children made me wonder whether I was
even qualified to speak to parents in grief. I was so convinced
that this was a wrong choice on the spirits' part that I asked
them to use my talents in any way *except* for communicating
messages from those who left life early. I was truly reluctant to
accept their constant presence in my life and my work. "No, no,
no," I said. But the kids on the other side said, "Yes, yes, yes!"
So I started to listen and, finally, *learn* from them. The love
and hope they've brought to their grieving families through my
work as a medium has transformed lives one by one . . . including mine.

Now I'm glad that they were persistent. Kids can really
be relentless when they want something and this persistence
doesn't diminish with death either. That's one of the things I
love about them.

In essence, kids in heaven have turned the tables on us. We
might have thought that we were intended to teach them about
life, protect them from the big, bad world, and turn the future
over to them when we're done here ourselves. But, in truth,
they're teaching *us* a few things.

The kids' perspective on Life (with a capital "L") is nothing short of transformational.

However, all of this life-changing talk can be tough for those of us on this side to take, especially if the loss is a recent one. So I hope that the way that I'm presenting their messages in this book makes them all a little easier to understand and embrace.

Each chapter and subject is broken down into four parts:

SpiritTweets are brief but thought-provoking quotes from the mouths of young people in spirit. In the same way that kids on earth are enjoying new ways to stay in touch with their friends and loved ones at all times, kids in spirit are frequently finding ways to stay connected with us too. These sudden and often surprising messages are the spiritual equivalent of texting or twittering; however, spirit messages tend to be packed with a lot more meaning than earthly ones. A SpiritTweet, as presented in this book, can be a daily reminder for us to look at everyday life from a more heavenly perspective.

SpiritThoughts provide an expanded discussion of the chapter's subject, including observations, thoughts, and stories about the spirits and people I've met. This segment also offers insight into how my personal life and my work as a medium intersect and inform each other.

SpiritAnswers provide the complete 411 on FAQs. Wherever I go in the United States and around the world, I am often asked the same questions. Some of my favorites get answered here. (Maybe yours are among them.)

SpiritSummary A pithy synopsis of the chapter's main points. Some people will come to this book looking for specific words of comfort, others for a more general understanding. Some will read it from cover to cover; others will home in on the answers to just their most pressing questions. Many will even revisit it later to be reminded of the words that spoke to them most profoundly. Whatever way *you* choose to approach this material, these summaries are designed to help guide your reading so it is a truly healing and empowering experience.

Finally, it might be assumed that because this book is about heavenly kids, that only someone who has lost a child will discover something of value in its pages, but please know that it is important to me, and to those whose messages I convey, that there is something of value for *everyone* in this book. It is our sincerest hope that these pages resonate strongly with those who have felt the loss of a young one directly, but we also hope and expect that countless other people will find meaning and answers here too.

In fact, a friend shared a story with me recently that reflects exactly why this book is such important reading for us *all*. When she first heard that her mother had been diagnosed with pancreatic cancer at age sixty-nine, she began sobbing. "Mom, please don't die on me," she pleaded. With the grace and wisdom of age, her mother simply replied, "Now Nancy, your father and I have had good lives—we've lived to see our children grow up to be fine adults. I can die happy." These words, of course, reaffirm what we all know to be true—it doesn't matter whether one's kids are toddlers or in their sixties, no parent wants to outlive them. Losing our young is just not the natural order of things. But this story also reminds us of something else, something kids in spirit say to me all the time: *everyone* will outlive *someone* they love at some point in time. That's just the way of life and death. Knowing more about how we live in the afterlife can help us change the way we look at death, and can potentially help us change the way we live our lives during our time here on earth too. That's what the children of all ages in spirit talk about. And that's the message they want to share with us all today.

Every time I hear from a kid in spirit, I'm profoundly touched. The young talk about life (and death) in such an open and honest way. No subject, including abortion and suicide, is taboo to them. They speak about the essentials of life—the things that affect each and every one of us.

I'm in awe of the way kids in spirit get right to the heart of the matter. *Are we loved? If we are, why do we feel so alone sometimes? How can we get through loss and heartbreak (of any kind)?*

We were all kids once, so hearing from these young ones reminds us of what it is like to feel invincible (and yet not to be). They've already gotten to the place where we're all going, so they have lots to tell us about what to expect there.

What can kids tell us about the afterlife that would help us live a better life here on earth? The answer is "plenty."

I have witnessed it time and again—young people living in spirit have a unique ability to deliver wisdom with humor and a lightness that can illuminate the path for all of us.

As it says in Isaiah 11:6, "and a little child shall lead them."

So, if you're ready, let's be led together.

HOLLISTER RAND

I'm Not
Dead,
I'm
DIFFERENT

This Is What It's Like to Be Dead?

What Kids Say about Death and the Afterlife

Spirit TWEET

"Heaven is a state of mind." (From a nineteen-year-old in spirit who struggled here on earth with depression.)

Spirit THOUGHTS

Could This Be Heaven?

So this *is what it's like to be dead,* I thought. A bright white light hovered in front of my face, diffused yet blinding at the same time. Hazy figures in blue and white moved with purpose at the periphery of my vision. Murmuring voices sounded urgent, but the words were indistinct. An insistent and annoying beeping cut through the human sounds. I couldn't move my legs, and my arms felt heavy and pinned back. My head wouldn't turn. I tried blinking my eyes rapidly, but the haziness didn't clear. No pearly gates. No Saint Peter. Could I be in the wrong place? If this was heaven, I didn't like it so far.

I started to take inventory. *Can I breathe? Yes. Can I wiggle my toes? Yes. Can I speak? No words came. Do I know how I got here? No. Do I know exactly where I am? No.*

Just when I thought that things couldn't get worse, I felt a sheet covering my face. *So I am dead! But wait, I'm aware of things going on around me.*

I started to take inventory again. *Can I wiggle my fingers? Yes. Swallow? Yes.* The beeping got louder. And then I heard . . .

"Welcome back."

At that point I still wasn't sure what I was being welcomed back to. It was only when the sheet was gently pulled away from my face that things became more clear. I was in a hospital emergency room. It was later explained to me that I had been in a severe one-car accident. My mother had broken her neck and survived. The car had been totaled and I had been nearly totaled too. I was eighteen years old. My father and sister had almost lost half their family in just under a second. After weeks in the hospital, I was rehabilitated and then sent on to my first year of college in three braces and an eye patch.

The journey back from what I thought was death was arduous and long. What I didn't realize then was that this journey was really a path to discovering what was *beyond* death. From the moment that sheet was removed from my face, I couldn't ignore the fact that I had been changed. Not just physically, but in sensitivity and awareness. Although I had seen ghosts and spirits from a young age, I'd always done my best to hide those experiences. I had wanted to be like most other people, not someone who found it difficult to tell the difference between the living and the dead.

Nearly dying changed my mind, however. It made me want to chat up *anyone* who could help me answer all my burgeoning questions. I had lived comfortably in a suburb of New York City all my life and it was a happy existence, but all of a sudden I found myself wondering, "Did life have a purpose?" And more specifically, "Did *my* life have a purpose?" I knew that the answer was "yes," to both questions. I just wasn't clear what that purpose might be. The accident made my family look at life differently, too. We all felt grateful that our situation didn't have an alternate outcome. During my stay at the hospital we saw that many other families weren't nearly as lucky.

In the years following the accident, I became driven to find answers to the even broader questions of life, too, such as "Where have we come from?" and "Where are we going?" and, the biggest question of all, "Why?"

Have I found all the answers? No. But I do keep searching. During the last twenty years of actively engaging with ghosts and spirits of all kinds, I've learned a lot about the afterlife. I've also discovered that whenever I think I've got it all figured out, those in spirit show me something new.

One thing I know for sure is that if we're willing to learn, there's no end to what those in spirit can teach us.

Benjamin Franklin famously said, "But in this world nothing can be said to be certain, except death and taxes!" This is more than just a statement of the obvious. It is a pairing of two truths that few of us are really willing to face. I, for one, get extensions on my taxes. I don't file until the last possible minute. And I'm not alone in that procrastination.

Most of us treat death in the same way. We don't want to deal with it until we have to. But death has a very rude way of interfering with our routines. People die sometimes without any warning at all. And death is at its most impolite when it disrupts our beliefs about how life is supposed to be. Children, for instance, are not supposed to die before their parents, but they do.

One of the many things I learned from meeting death in an up close and personal way is not to make any assumptions about the dying experience and what life is like after death. If, in fact, death is a certainty for us all, and youth is no guard against it, we should gather as much information about it from the people living on the other side of life as we can. And that is exactly what I do.

Thankfully, the possibility of dying in that car crash didn't scare me as much as it might have scared most others because I had already met many people who had died and "survived," so to speak. In fact, my ability to communicate with the spirits over the years had actually given me a bit of an advantage. I figured that if they had made it through their experience, I could make it through mine.

All-Night Slumber Parties

For as long as I can remember, spirits were part of my life . . . a big part. During my youth there was no clear dividing line between the seen and the unseen worlds. Whatever division there might have been blurred completely at night when the spirits appeared as if in 3-D Technicolor.

Once the lights were out, they simply showed up.

This wasn't always a pleasant experience for me, especially when I was very young. And it definitely wasn't one I felt confident sharing. Of course my parents knew that something was up; I was obsessed with ghost stories and had created elaborate escape plans in the event my room became too crowded with these visitors. My strategies included climbing out of my second-story bedroom window using a collapsible ladder stored under my bed. Night-lights burned from dusk until dawn and still, the spirits came.

Visits from Pop-Pop

During my earliest years, I treasured one comfort even more than my angora blue blanket: the love of my grandfather.

Pop-Pop, as he was affectionately called, was a man among women in our family. He had raised three girls—my mother and her two sisters—during a challenging time in our country's history, the Depression. His work as a master electrician kept food on the table at a time when many had nothing. By the time I was born, he had lost most of his hair except for the white fringe above his ears. He had a fair Scottish complexion with eyes that seemed all the more blue because of his ruddy cheeks. My grandfather made me feel special, but more important, he made me feel . . . safe.

Pop-Pop died of heart failure when I was barely of school age. I was kept away from the funeral home, service, and burial because my parents thought I was too young. A caring family friend (who was also my Sunday school teacher) stayed with me while all the others dealt with the details of death.

This family friend told me that Pop-Pop had gone to live in heaven. She did her best to help me understand this sudden change in my reality. But what she didn't understand was that my reality hadn't changed as much as she had thought.

From the day my grandfather died, he visited with me. In fact, the night my parents were greeting people at the funeral home, Pop-Pop stood at the foot of my bed and then he kissed me on the forehead. Whenever Pop-Pop was around, all the other spirits stayed away, except for one, a boy my own age.

I could tell that Pop-Pop and this little boy were happy being together. The boy didn't say anything, but I got a good look at him. His hair had a reddish tint, his eyes were blue, and he glanced away, shyly.

When I told my mother about seeing Pop-Pop and the little boy, I thought that she would be happy. Instead, she didn't want to talk about it. It was at that moment that I first realized it might not be okay to see people others thought were dead, and worst of all, talk about it! I knew that there was something different about me, and that difference wasn't necessarily desirable. It was then that I started doing my best to ignore the constant presence of the spirits in my life.

Years later I found out that the little boy Pop-Pop brought to meet me was my uncle who had died at the age of six. His middle name was Gibson and his nickname was "Gibby." His death caused my grandmother's hair to turn white overnight (or so my mother said). My grandmother's grief was so great that she couldn't even return to the house where Gibby had lived. My mother was sent away for the summer while my grandfather set up a new house for the family, the house where my grandmother eventually died at the age of seventy-six.

The only photo we have of Gibby is one in which he is smiling shyly, a perfect chubby little hand held up to his face, his head tilted down and his one bare leg bent inward at the knee in a physical aw-shucks expression. This is exactly as he looked when Pop-Pop brought him to my bedside.

Gibby was the first heavenly child I had ever met. He was the first of many to come.

Living Big in the Great Beyond

So what is it like to be dead? Well, that depends on who you talk to. After my own brush with death, I spent many years speaking with spirits from various religious and ethnic backgrounds. As a result I understand that there are as many descriptions of life in the afterlife (and names for heaven) as there are spirits who dwell there. But while the details of each person's experience may be different, there is an underlying consistency in the way things work. Life beyond death is more expansive and magnificent than we can imagine. Fortunately, those in spirit, especially the kids, present the sometimes lofty and powerful concepts of life-after-death in an accessible and succinct way.

One young man in spirit told me, "There are many different neighborhoods here. I don't visit the bad ones, because I like being with nice people." Hmmm . . . well this sounded like good advice to me. Especially since earlier in my life (when I didn't know any better), I had met some unsavory people in spirit during "ghost busting" and haunted house adventures. Thanks to that young spirit, I learned that I could set parameters for my encounters. Now only those who live in the neighborhood of love are welcomed to visit me.

Because I stay out of the afterlife's "bad" neighborhoods, my interest and frame of reference for spirit communication comes from a loving perspective. The spirits I talk to are interested in helping us heal from grief. They give us hints for living a better life here and they help prepare us for living in heaven ourselves one day.

Living in heaven. That is the first thing that those in spirit want us to know. They're *living*, not dead.

Jacob's Fast Comeback

Several years ago, an entire family—mother, father, son and daughter—came to see me. As they were sitting down, a young man in spirit who looked to be in his late teens caught my eye as he started running around the room. He was so fast that he was a blur. While running by, he gave me the name, Jacob. I said to the family, "There's a young man named Jacob here, and boy, does he run fast!" The mother started to cry, the father put his head in his hands, the brother looked like he was going to bolt out of the room, and the sister said, "My brother who died is named Jacob, and he was a runner in high school." Jacob went on to speak to each member of his family, even giving his brother a hard time about his schoolwork. (He used to do the same thing before he died, his brother told me.) Then all of a sudden, with no warning, Jacob's father started weeping and blurted out, "He's dead and gone." Without missing a beat, Jacob shouted in my ear, "I'm *not* dead and gone: I'm . . . *different.*" I thought to myself, *Well, that says it all, and if I ever write a book, that will be the title.*

Jacob's father's cry of despair is easy to understand. When someone close to us dies, it seems as though death is the end of life, relationship, legacy, and hope. We don't want our loved ones in spirit to be "different," we want them to be *here.* However, the spirits look at death from a different perspective, one that can seem very alien to us. *So how do the spirits view death, especially the young ones?* Well, death is nothing more to them than transportation to the other side of life.

At first it might seem strange to liken something as momentous as death to a car, boat, plane, or train ride. But kids in spirit, like kids on earth, are less interested in the trip and more interested in the destination. Anyone who has ever been on the road with kids knows that! "Are we there yet?" is the question that every kid asks on the way. When I speak to the young in spirit, they consistently avoid describing the way they died. This is very frustrating for me, because I'm nosy by nature and maybe more important, because getting details about a passing makes me feel like I'm doing my job. Early on in my work as a professional medium, a spirit in his early twenties came to visit a group circle. One of the first questions I asked him was, "How did you die?" He responded, "I was hit on the head with a hammer." Well! That raised all sorts of questions for me! I wanted to know if it had been some sort of freak accident or if he had been purposely hit on the head with the hammer. His reply? "That's just how I got here." How irritating! I wanted details and he viewed his death as simply . . . the route from point A to point B.

On the other hand, when I speak to spirits who passed at a ripe old age, they often tell me about every doctor's visit, every blood test, and every ache and pain. When I ask why it's different with kids, I get some very logical answers. First of all, those who suffered with physical ailments for a time before passing tell me that their dying process becomes part of their life experience. Because most kids (with some exceptions, of course) tend not to have to deal with the gradual disintegration of the body, their frame of reference is different. Many of the kids I talk to in spirit have actually died while in motion.

The Fearless Factor

Kids, on the whole, don't have a sense of mortality. Death doesn't really factor into the way they approach life. Kids don't really think about their own deaths. They think that they're going to live forever . . . and, in a sense, they're right.

But the most loving and profound reason that the young in spirit don't concentrate on the details of their deaths is because it reinforces the pain that those they love are feeling over their loss. Any information they do provide is often shared to allay the fears of friends and relatives. For instance, a teenage girl who was run off the road by a drunk driver told her mother that she was so busy trying to steer the car that she didn't have a moment of fear. The next thing she knew, her beloved grandmother in spirit was there to take her hand.

Kids in spirit aren't interested in perpetuating *our* stories of *their* deaths. Those left behind can become so obsessed about the mode of transportation (the accident, the murder, the suicide) that they can't even consider the destination. Kids, on the other hand, are more interested in what happens after they arrive than in how they got there.

Spirit Multitasking

Often I'm asked during a session, "Is my loved one happy in heaven?" Interestingly enough, I've never had a spirit reply, "Yes." I was a little concerned about this until I learned from the spirits that our idea of happiness here on earth just doesn't translate to the experience of the afterlife. Here on this side of life, being happy is often related to outside circumstances as in, "I'm so happy that I got a raise," or, "You make me so very happy." The spirits talk about peace rather than happiness. What I've learned from spirits is that the dead have peace— and based on what I can see, they're definitely not resting in it.

From the viewpoint of those in spirit, there's a lot going on in heaven. Life in the afterlife is busy. According to the spirits things happen instantaneously in a way that time on earth doesn't allow. Although it may be difficult for us to understand, this sense of living in the fast lane delights the spirits, especially the young ones. Kids on earth are often heard to say, "Higher, faster. Do it again!" Kids in heaven embrace the speed of the afterlife as their natural state of being. One teenager told his parents through me that in heaven things happened as fast as he wanted them to. His parents confirmed that their son was incredibly impatient and was always complaining that he wanted life to move faster. In fact, he had died while driving well over the speed limit in his new car.

What makes such speed possible in the afterlife is that the spirits aren't subject to the physical limitations that we are. They can be in multiple locations at once because a physical body no longer contains them. In many sessions, loved ones in spirit have indicated that they are aware of what's taking place in the lives of numerous people still living on earth. In one instance during a session, a teenager in spirit mentioned each family member's morning's activities. When the family conferred with one another, they were astonished to discover that these activities had taken place *at the same time*! I just know that the teenager did it to see their reaction! Teenagers are like that—they just want to make an impact.

Not being limited by a physical body opens up all sorts of possibilities for kids in spirit. One young boy who was about five or six started singing "It's a Small World" to me and showed me a movie of the Disneyland ride in my mind. He told me that he's riding the ride for real now in heaven and gets to visit all the other countries in the land of spirit. His parents laughed through their tears as they told me that their son couldn't get enough of that ride when they visited Disneyland on a family vacation. As soon as the last chorus had been sung, he wanted to start at the beginning again. Well, now he doesn't have to get off that ride.

Although the majority of children who visit me from heaven were perfectly healthy when they left the earth, I've also communicated with many who suffered with various congenital or terminal illnesses before dying. These kids leave all their suffering behind when they pass. One of the more stunning connections I experienced was with a girl who visited with her mother at a group event. For some reason, she wouldn't let me see what she looked like, but she gave me her name, Anna, and I could feel her presence. She also had a very sharp mind and started to impress me with philosophical thoughts and scientific theories. When Anna finally paused in her message, her mother leapt to her feet and exclaimed, "I knew she was perfect!" Anna's mother went on to explain to the group that her daughter had been mentally impaired while on earth. Despite those limitations, Anna's mother, who had a PhD in philosophy, wanted to share what she loved with her daughter. So night after night, instead of reading children's stories to Anna, she read philosophy and science books. She always believed that her daughter understood everything, even though she couldn't express it. Anna, in spirit, demonstrated that her mother was right.

After I communicate with a child in heaven who can now run freely when he couldn't walk on earth, I imagine that wheelchairs, crutches, oxygen tanks, and hospital beds are all lined up outside the gates of heaven like strollers outside a ride at Disneyland. Fanciful, I know, but it illustrates the fact that children who suffered here can finally leave that physical suffering behind. In fact, *all* of us who suffer here will leave that physical suffering behind.

A Light Tale from Richard

I'm writing this chapter while in Sedona, Arizona. From my window, I can see the red rocks rising up to the sky. As the sun sets, the red becomes richer and the beige turns to gold. The colors are deeper and more intense and the light radiates more brightly here than just about anywhere else I know . . . except heaven. A young man in spirit named Richard agrees with me. While I was on the phone with his mother, Richard was emphatic about how much light there is in heaven. His mother laughed when I told her that Richard wanted her to know, without a doubt, that he was "living in the light." After the session was over, Richard's mom told me that they used to call him, "the mushroom," because he chose their darkened basement for a bedroom rather than a beautiful, sunny space upstairs. The family used to joke with him about "living in the light." Richard's preference for the dark may be a bit unusual. For the most part, kids on earth don't love the dark so when in spirit, they often reassure their parents that they're no longer afraid of the dark. Their fear is gone, because there simply isn't any darkness where they are now. There is no need for night-lights in heaven.

Since heaven is a land of light, there's no night and day. And without night and day, there is also no sense of the passage of time. Spirits live in the eternal *now*. For the most part, kids living in heaven don't mention time at all, unless it is in reference to an upcoming birthday. Birthdays are a big subject because they are important to kids on earth, so kids in spirit naturally enjoy acknowledging these memories. During a session, a fourteen-year-old boy in heaven reminded his mother to bake a German chocolate cake for his birthday, which was coming soon. He then gave me what looked like a homemade Valentine's Day card. His mother responded with, "Oh yes, he loved that cake. I baked it for his birthday every year, which is on Valentine's Day."

Other dates that are important to us, such as holidays, anniversaries, and the date of one's passing are also mentioned by those in spirit. In my experience, kid spirits like to talk about holidays, whereas those who pass later in life often bring up wedding anniversaries and the dates on which they passed.

The date and time that someone passes is of great importance to us. Therefore, it is very common for those in spirit to mention the care they might have taken in choosing when to pass. Many report that they tried to wait for someone to arrive at the hospital, or even that they wanted to live long enough for a wedding or other such family celebration to take place. A high school senior with brain cancer named Brian had another, very important reason to hold on to life. During a group event he told me that he tried his best to live past midnight to avoid dying on his girlfriend Ashley's birthday. This was confirmed by his mother who said that Brian had lived until 12:03 a.m. the morning *after* Ashley's birthday. Even though Brian was unconscious at the time of his passing, all who were gathered by his bed at the hospital just knew he was waiting until the stroke of midnight.

Although there are no calendars and clocks in heaven, the spirits respond to our way of organizing day-to-day life. Clocks

and watches are mentioned f
cate, especially if the items w
evening of spirit communic
husband in spirit flashed a
with the time stopped a
Beverly, that although
like a watch when he died, ..
group that before coming to the even,
in her hand, which had indeed stopped at 3:12.

One of the differences between talking with kids
grown-ups in heaven is that kids talk about music, cell phones,
and video games instead of clocks and watches. Kids are particularly good at communicating *directly* with loved ones using
music and electronic devices. For a more in-depth discussion
of how kids communicate from the other side, take a look at
chapter 10: "Bringing Heaven Home—How Kids Say 'Hi' from
the Other Side."

E-viting Spirit Friends to the Party

*So if there aren't calendars and watches in heaven, how do those
in spirit manage to show up on time to an appointment their loved
ones have made with a medium?* Well, very simply, they do so
because *you* set the intention that a connection is going to take
place. Your thoughts are like "e-vites" that get sent to the right
heavenly in-box.

My most memorable example of how this works was when
I met with Nancy, a young woman who was one of the last
remaining members of her family line. At the start of our
time together, I noticed a large group of spirits standing behind her, young and old alike. Names started popping into my

elyn, Jackie, Betsy, Allen," and the list went

es!" Nancy exclaimed. "These are all my rela-

o catch my breath before going on with the list of

vas like roll call. When the session was over, I told

hat I had never had this kind of thing happen before.

eemed surprised. "I just did what you told me to do before

session. I started thinking about my loved ones in spirit. But

then I thought that it might even be better if I actually wrote out invitations for each of them with a request to RSVP. Three days ago I reminded them about the RSVP." I was really taken aback. No one had done that before. The spirits obviously knew that she was serious!

My experience with Nancy's *entire* family illustrates that not only are the spirits open to our invitations to communicate, but that their visits are coordinated with one another. As each spirit stepped up to give his or her name, they were not only relating to Nancy and me, but to one another.

Spirits in heaven live in relationship there, much as we do here. Relationship bonds don't dissolve with death, but divisions caused by misunderstanding and judgment do. Death allows the masks, the illusions, and the limitations of life on earth to drop away. Dying doesn't necessarily bring immediate and complete enlightenment, but it does allow us to see ourselves as we really are. While we're here on the earth, our perceptions are colored by the filters of values, personal and religious beliefs, and who we'd *like* ourselves to be. In heaven, we can't fall back on illusions or self-delusion. All aspects of ourselves, past, present, and even future reside in the eternal now of the afterlife. This truth was stated best by a dear friend, Brett, who died by falling off a balcony in France when he was thirty-three. When a group of friends who were also mediums got together, we all heard Brett say, "I have met my many selves."

Living in the afterlife not only gives us the opportunity to meet all of the aspects of ourselves, but it also helps us to feel the effect that our thoughts, words, deeds, and our dying have had on *everyone* we knew during our life on earth.

That's a sobering thought, I know, and a bit overwhelming to grasp. However, it sure gives spirits a compelling reason to reach out from heaven to help heal the pain created when death stepped in.

Spirit ANSWERS

Are the "other side," the "afterlife," and "heaven" all the same place?

I use the "other side" and the "afterlife" interchangeably to include all aspects and areas of life outside of the physical body. It is important to remember that these are earthly words, however. The spirits don't necessarily see their lives as "afterlives" or themselves as living on the "other side" of anything. They're just alive.

The spirits have shown me different places on the "other side," some which are very wonderful and some which are neighborhoods I prefer to never visit again. Therefore, I work very much at the love vibration where those who are loved and have loved dwell. I'm comfortable with using the word "heaven" because I grew up going to church. Many of my clients use the word to describe where they believe their loved ones in spirit dwell, and some spirits have reinforced that concept.

Spirits do their best to convey their living reality. However,

I know that when they talk about their lives, they present things in ways that I and their loved ones can understand. On occasion, I've spoken with spirits who show me worlds that are beyond anything that we can imagine here on earth. Mathematical and geometric patterns overlay a broad, expansive place where light and sound create a latitude and longitude. I know all of this sounds like babbling. That's because much of what I've seen I can't even begin to decipher. Simply put, the life beyond this one is expansive beyond our comprehension and can't be readily or completely described. Any words that we use to define life after death very likely limit and diminish its magnificence.

Is heaven a lot like earth?

This is like asking if New York is like Tokyo or if London is like Bangkok. Buildings are buildings and people are people wherever you go, but they often look and act differently in different places. The same is true in heaven. Life continues there, but the customs vary greatly!

From glimpses I've been shown of various realms of the spirit world, there are some things that are indescribable. For the most part, though, our loved ones in spirit talk about heaven in terms that we can grasp and understand.

For example, in a session with a beautiful young widow named Galina, her husband in spirit, Vince, said, "I'm building the dream house you always wanted." He projected three images into my mind of an estate that looked quite a bit like Tara in *Gone with the Wind*. Galina clapped her hands with delight and said, "That's the house he promised to build for me!" Vince was studying to be an architect when he died in a freak accident on his summer job building houses. Being inquisitive (as I always am), I asked him if there are builders in heaven. He informed me, "No, I just think about a house and it is there." Here on earth, everything created begins with a thought and then we go through the process of working to make things happen. In heaven, though, thought creates reality—immediately! Consider this. Heaven is always in the process of being created, changed, and transformed by the spirits living there.

Spirits talk about cities in heaven, sometimes in what seems like magical terms. Dustin, a young aspiring actor, dreamed of moving from a small Midwestern town to New York City. After his death in a car crash shortly before his eighteenth birthday, Dustin found himself in a magnificent city that defied description. Instead of using words, Dustin gave me quick flashes of his heavenly city. It had lots of theaters, of course. However, what astounded me most was the image of thin, towering, shiny golden skyscrapers, taller than any we could build on earth. Everything glowed with light, and although there was no obvious electrical grid, there was the sense of a powerful energy source.

What is the landscape like?

Spirits describe colorful gardens, mountains with peaks reaching beyond the clouds, rivers that flow gently and are always stocked with fish, placid lakes that reflect the colors of the rainbow, and oceans stretching into eternity. Although extraordinarily lush, all is in order. A daughter in spirit who had been studying to be a landscape architect before she passed told her mother that she loved the gardens in heaven because no weeding was necessary! (Guess I won't be packing a Weed-wacker in my coffin.)

Heaven is big, too. When a father in spirit was asked by his daughter what he did with his time, he said, "I'm walking the property lines." I thought that this was a strange response until his daughter told me that he used to spend every evening walking the property lines of their ranch in Texas. Her father then went on to say, "I've been doing a lot of walking over here and so far haven't found the end of heaven."

Can I ski or surf there?

We might like to think of our loved ones "resting in peace." Actually, this couldn't be further from the truth. Spirits are active! Richie, a twenty-two-year-old who died in a skiing accident, couldn't wait to tell his sister that, in spirit, he had finally mastered the jump. Snowboarders, ice-skaters, mountain climbers, skateboarders, and surfers in spirit have talked about doing what they love on the other side. In a way, I enjoy living vicariously through them; the closest I've ever come to skiing is sipping hot chocolate in an Alpine lodge.

What if I don't like everyone there? Can I avoid people I don't care for?

Remember the saying, "Birds of a feather flock together"? Well, this is true for the spirit world perhaps more than anywhere else! Those with similar thoughts, family ties, and love bonds are able to be together once again in spirit. The opposite is also true—those whose actions have hurt others here on the earth remain with their own kind until they change. I'm convinced that this is one of the reasons why those in spirit desire to communicate through mediums. They have the opportunity to acknowledge their actions to those left behind on earth.

In thinking about this question, I remembered a stepfather in spirit named Frank, who appeared for his stepdaughter, Sarah, during a group session. Frank asked permission to speak with Sarah. At first, I wasn't sure that she was going to agree. She curled up in her chair, almost in a fetal position. Frank, a tall man with strawberry blond hair and blue eyes, told Sarah that he was so sorry for how he had treated her. He could see now how wrong he was and had to face himself and his deeds. Frank was holding a baby who he told me had passed by abortion. He kept repeating, "I'm so sorry." Sarah acknowledged Frank's contrition. Her body began to relax and she sat up straight and strong in her chair.

I later learned that Sarah's stepfather had sexually abused her from ages twelve to sixteen. He had impregnated her and the baby was aborted. Several months after the message from her stepfather, Sarah's husband gave my assistant a message for me, in person. Sarah's husband is a big man, tall and muscle-bound. His stature is a bit intimidating; he's definitely someone you want on your side. He told my assistant that Sarah was a different person after receiving that message from her father. The specter of abuse that had haunted her for years was finally gone. Not only could Sarah embrace life in a different way here, she is no longer afraid of seeing her stepfather in the spirit world. Then with tears in his eyes, this big, powerful man told my assistant that even if I never did another thing here on earth, I had earned angel's wings. Each morning I check in the mirror to see if those wings are sprouting. So far, there's not even a feather. I guess this means that my work isn't done yet.

Are there cliques in heaven?

Fortunately, heaven isn't like high school, where jocks and cheerleaders all hang out together. There are no "in" groups to join. Heaven is a place where who you are at your core is all you have. The irony of it is that those living at the highest vibration in the spirit world are not even interested in flaunting their position. In fact, the higher we rise in the spirit world, the less position matters to us.

Is there such a thing as "status" in heaven?

Having the biggest bank account on earth doesn't guarantee you the best table in heaven. Our reservation is secured by the totality of our thoughts, words, and actions on the earthly plane. The status symbols we value here, like mansions and fine cars, are available to us in the spirit world, but they are expressions of thought and there is no struggle to earn them. Think of it this way: the spirit world is like the reflection of a palatial resort in a still mountain lake. What is grand and expensive on solid land is turned upside down and floats on the surface; it looks real, but it isn't. Dying is like diving through the reflection of earthly things. Living in the spirit world is like being immersed in the cool waters of love, peace, and joy while being able to enjoy the reflection of the things we enjoyed on earth.

What if I get caught in limbo? Or make a wrong turn and end up in hell? Can I work my way to heaven eventually?

The good news is that you don't need a GPS to find your way to heaven, even if you can't get out of your driveway without it! The reason you don't need to worry is because family members and guides serve as a heavenly welcoming committee. No one dies alone or is ever abandoned.

Now that's not to say that there isn't a "limbo" state of sorts. Some spirits get themselves stuck in a rut because of their own beliefs about death as well as their refusal to give up intense emotions such as rage, blame, and guilt. I've even met spirits who refuse to accept that they're dead! This seems particularly prevalent in situations where there isn't an opportunity for a spirit to see himself separating from the body. Don't let this freak you out, though, because mediums help spirits in "limbo" with what we call rescue circles, a cooperative effort between mediums on earth and guiding spirits in the afterlife. It is easy to think of the function of rescue circles in terms of airline travel. When a traveler arrives at a massive international airport, he may be a bit confused and disoriented. People from all countries are walking around and heading to different destinations. If he didn't see a relative or friend at the gate (even though that person was there waiting), the traveler might start wandering around trying to figure out where to go by following signs in the airport. However, the language is different in this foreign country and he doesn't understand what people are saying to him. Fortunately, with a medium present as an interpreter, the language of spirit begins to make sense. Guiding spirits are like VIP airport guides who will take the traveler to the proper gate for his connecting flight. This guide also relieves the traveler of his luggage, because it is no longer needed.

There's one more thing to keep in mind about the transition

between worlds, though. Our dying experience can often be influenced by final thoughts. There is a Buddhist belief that the way someone enters the afterlife is *determined* by this last thought. The importance of last thoughts (ours and those of the people around us) has been emphasized by the spirits time and again. A young man suffering with leukemia told me that he heard singing as he was dying. His last thoughts were of God's love and he was spirited away in harmony. His mother confirmed that several members of her church choir were singing hymns right outside his hospital room. Because her son was unconscious at the time of his passing, she didn't think that he could hear the music. Just because the body can't express consciousness, doesn't mean that the spirit isn't fully conscious. All the loving words and thoughts we share with those who are dying helps them more than we may know.

Even people who die under extreme circumstances are helped by the love they've experienced during their lifetimes. I remember speaking with a young woman in spirit who had what we might think of as a difficult passing because she was raped and murdered. And yet, when she spoke with her parents from spirit, she said that the experience of dying was like a dream. The only thing real to her at the time of her death was the love she had always felt from her family and the face of her grandmother who was waiting for her on the other side.

When I first started working as a medium, I came across a quote by Philip Massinger that has inspired my life and work. He wrote, "Death has a thousand doors to let out life. I shall find one." What I realized during my search for that one door is that death also has a thousand doors to let life *in*. Last thoughts are like keys to the thousand doors. With keys of love, joy, and peace in your hands, the door to hell can't be opened by mistake because the keys just don't fit the lock.

Spirit SUMMARY

It can be devastating to lose someone we love, especially if death comes with no warning. When a child dies, the loss may feel unbearable and the questions innumerable. How can I go on without my child? Is he okay? Is there really life after death? Or is she gone forever? Kids in spirit try to ease our grief by reaching out from heaven to touch us with their love. By giving us a glimpse into an eternity that we all will share, kids in spirit introduce us to a world where life is experienced without limitations of time, age, disability, or pain.

2

Playing with Spirits

When Spirit Communication Works
(and When It Doesn't)

$\mathscr{S}pirit$ TWEET

"I like playing with you." (Statement made to me by a four-year-old boy in spirit who was "acting up" during a group event.)

$\mathscr{S}pirit$ THOUGHTS

Playing by the Rules

One of the reasons I like being around kids in spirit is that they like to play. What I've learned, though, is that they don't always like to play by the rules.

By rules, I mean the procedures my spirit helpers and I have worked out to make communication run smoothly. Speaking with spirits is an orderly process. That is, until kids get into the mix.

Just as I have event organizers who set up the chairs and check people in at the door, I have helper spirits who do the same on their side of things. When I'm about to do an event, I pray and confer with these helpers. These helpers line up spirits in an orderly fashion. Then when the time is right, they direct my attention to the next spirit in line. The spirit stands near or behind a person in the audience. This system works very well. Without order, an event would be chaotic. Spirits would be vying for my attention and yelling out orders like brokers on the floor of the stock exchange. I would be too overwhelmed by the cacophony of sound generated by them collectively to be able to discern clear messages from any individual spirit.

Well, sometimes kids in spirit just don't like to wait in line.

At a small group event, as we were about to close, a boy in spirit who looked to be about four started running around in circles right in the center of the room. He wasn't doing any of the things that well-behaved spirits do, such as stand behind the person to whom he belonged or refrain from saying anything until a helper guide gives the okay. I didn't know what to do about this little guy, so I asked him what *he* liked to do. "I like going to the zoo." Well, good. That was a start. "Is there anyone here that you go to the zoo with?" I asked. (I thought I was being clever and could figure out who he belonged to from his answer.) "A boy from my class," he responded. That didn't help me much.

Finally, I just started to describe him to the group, hoping that someone would claim him. No response. Between sprints around the room, he gave me two names, Jared and Sarah. A lady in the group perked up. "My two children are named Jared and Sarah," she said. Then all the bits of information started making sense. Her son, Jared, had recently visited their local zoo with his class. Two years previously, Jared's friend and preschool classmate had died. Since then, Jared had been telling his mother that his friend still came to play with him. His mother assumed that Jared's friend was imaginary. We learned that day that Jared's friend was anything *but* imaginary. Right before ending the event, I received one of the greatest compliments ever. This little spirit boy who hadn't stopped moving from the moment he appeared, paused, and said, "I like playing with you." In my mind I answered, "I like playing with you, too."

Even though kids don't always like to play by the rules, as a medium, it is important to know what the rules are. There are three tiers to consider:

1. The general laws of the universe that also govern spirit communication.
2. The functional rules of making a good connection with spirits.
3. The guidelines each medium sets up to help make spirit communication consistent.

This is easier to understand if we think of it in terms of the American governmental system. Here in the United States, there are federal laws that govern all of us, state laws that are enforced only within state lines, and local laws that are applied in smaller incorporated or unincorporated areas. At no time can a state or local law be in opposition to a federal law. For instance, Indiana, Florida, and New York can't suddenly decide that everyone in their states must drive on the left side of the road. Chaos would reign. However, each state has sovereignty in other matters.

As a medium, if you operate in opposition to the general

laws of the universe, chaos will reign in your life because, in a sense, you will be driving into oncoming traffic. I've had a number of budding spirit communicators in my development workshops for whom this was true. Fortunately, once someone learns the laws and is willing to abide by them, order is restored.

In this analogy, the state laws would be the physical rules for connecting to spirit. This includes the practical ways that every medium sees, hears, feels, smells, and tastes what remains unnoticed by most other people.

Local laws are the guidelines that each medium sets up with their spirit helpers as an organizational tool and shorthand to make the process of communication much easier.

One of the ways that mediums learn the laws, rules, and guidelines of spirit communication is to meet with other mediums for development circles. Before I ever gave messages in front of groups, I attended these meetings week after week. I did this for *years*.

When those in spirit finally thought that I was prepared to work in public, I was asked to do a presentation for a metaphysical organization in Anaheim, California. The evening went very well and I was greatly encouraged because the same organization asked me to come again.

During the following week's development circle, I thanked the helper spirits for all they had done with me during the event. I told them that I looked forward to collaborating with them again. At that point several people in the room got the message that a trainee helper spirit was going to join me at the next event. "A *trainee*?" I practically screamed. "I need a professional!" The thought of getting up in front of a group of people with a helper spirit who had as little experience as I was *not* appealing.

Once I calmed down, a medium in the group gave me another message from the spirits. "Trust," they said. A member of that development circle gave me an ID bracelet with that very word engraved on it. I wore that bracelet every day for the next two years. In time, I learned to trust my connection to those in spirit.

Let me state very clearly that this isn't *blind* trust. This is trust built up over many years of relationship with those living in the unseen world. I am an active participant in creating guidelines with the spirits who communicate with me. The resulting confidence in the information I receive allows me to stand firm, whether the person on the receiving end understands or not.

Skeptics in the House

Tim was a man with a powerful presence. When he walked into the office for a session, he had an "I get my way" kind of gait. His wife, Barbara, followed him quietly into the room and they both sat down. As I quickly explained how the spirits work with me, I could feel the presence of a young man in spirit. He identified himself as their son. With each piece of information that came through, Barbara said, "Yes," or indicated that she understood what her son was communicating to me. Tim, on the other hand, sat with his arms crossed.

Up to this point, their son hadn't given me his name. He had provided details of his life including a description of the uniform he wore for his after-school job at the pizza place. Halfway through our meeting, Tim stopped me brusquely and said, "Does he give you a name?" Almost immediately, the name Michael came into my mind. When I shared the name, Tim replied, "I don't believe it. Some other medium we went to see gave us the name, Michael." Tim then went on to tell me the name of the other medium that he had seen, a well-respected medium who I knew personally. "Why can't you get our son's name, or at least the name of his best friend?" Tim asked. In response, I heard his son say, "Wait. You'll know what it means in a couple of days." Then his son laughed in my ear, but I couldn't understand the humor in his message. Why would a loving son give two separate mediums a name that didn't make any sense to his father?

The following weekend, when I looked out over the audience at a public event, Tim was sitting in the third row. His wife, Barbara, wasn't there. *Uh-oh*, I thought. During the evening, I didn't receive a message for Tim. Nor did he raise his hand to ask a question. When the event was over, I figured that I was home free. But as I started to walk out the door, I saw Tim striding toward me. He was a man with a mission and I braced myself for an uncomfortable encounter.

"Hollister, you won't believe this," he said. "I had some of my son's friends over to the house for pizza last night." Then he paused for dramatic effect. "The kids started talking about the pizza place and my son's best friend asked, 'What happened to Michael who worked my shift? He hasn't been around lately.'"

We stood there silently for a moment and then Tim said, "It's just like my son to try to get the best of me." Tim's son had coordinated quite a little prank and used two mediums to pull it off! He sent a communiqué to his skeptical father that he was still around and had a little fun with him just as he had done many times before he passed. That night before going to bed, I got the giggles about the whole thing. As I said before, kids in spirit don't always play by our rules!

One of my greatest challenges as a medium is handling the expectations of the people who come to see me. Early on I learned that everyone who goes to see a medium has an agenda. The agenda can be as simple as curiosity, or a plan to prove that communication is hogwash, or a desperate desire to connect with a son or daughter. So . . . I had to make a choice. Do I worry about the agendas of people, all of which can be different? Or, do I work with the laws of spirits, which are of a higher order? I've opted for playing by the laws of the spirit world.

This choice, however, doesn't exempt me from having to deal with those who question whether it is even possible to talk to the spirits.

When I was a little girl, well-meaning people, who I now realize were also skeptical *and* fearful, told me that I was imagining the spirits in my room at night. However, the spirits didn't seem to care if people thought they were real or not. They just kept coming night after night anyway. Ultimately, after many years of spirit experiences, I grew confident in presenting the reality of the spirit world despite the skepticism of those who haven't come face-to-face with spirits themselves.

Once I started appearing publicly as a medium, my work was met with broader skepticism, which sometimes led to dramatic encounters with skeptics. I vividly recall one event in Santa Monica, California, which occurred early in my career. Many spirits showed up for audience members that evening. *This is going well*, I thought, until a woman about thirty-five years of age with long, black hair stood up in the back of the room. She yelled out, "Nothing I've seen here today proves to me that there is life after death or that you can talk with the dead!" She was so angry that her face was red and her eyes shot daggers at me. Before I could respond, another young woman in the crowd stood up, spun around, faced the woman and said, "She [pointing to me] told me at another event that my mother was sorry that she had taken her own life when I was two years old. She also told me that my mother was encouraging me to deal with my depression so that I could make different choices. I told her [pointing to me again] that she was wrong because my mother died from ovarian cancer. But when I spoke to my grandmother, she confessed that my mother had committed suicide. My mother came to me in a dream and I know that she's going to help me. So don't tell me that there isn't life after death or that she [pointing to me yet again] isn't for real." These words hung in the air like laundry strung out to dry. Reflecting later, I recognized that two people, even if provided with much of the same evidence, can come to different conclusions depending upon their own fiercely held beliefs. A change in perspective is often the result of a direct and personal encounter with a loved one in spirit. It doesn't necessarily come by reading or observation alone.

That experience certainly helped me face skeptics later in my career with more assurance, but nothing could have prepared me for meeting a spirit skeptic. That's right, even the spirits can be skeptical at times, as I once discovered! I always assumed that if a spirit was talking to me, he believed in spirit communication. Not necessarily so. Years ago at a small event, a father in spirit said to his daughter, "I wouldn't be caught *dead* doing this [meaning talking through a medium]." The daughter laughed, saying that Dad had been a real skeptic and thought that her interest in psychics and mediums was for the birds. I responded to the father in spirit, "Sir, I regret to inform you that not only are you dead, but you're talking to a medium." He then proceeded to argue with me. "I'm *not* dead," he said. And I had to concede the point.

Interestingly enough, I haven't yet met a young person living in spirit who is skeptical. Kids make it seem as though living in heaven is natural for them. The longer we live on earth, the easier it is to forget that, at first, it felt unnatural living *here*. We had to learn how to eat, how to walk, how to read and write, in other words, how to live in a body. One afternoon, while I watched a toddler walking along with his grandfather, I noticed that they were walking *exactly* the same way—wobbly and unbalanced. It occurred to me that while one was getting used to having a body, the other was preparing to no longer being limited by it.

Afterlife Science

The growing popularity of spirit communication has garnered the interest of the scientific community. An entire branch of scientific inquiry, dubbed "afterlife science," is taking hold in universities around the country. I'm no stranger to the scientific way of approaching life because my father was a science teacher. He devoted his life to educating the young in the natural sciences. I've taken many a trek through the woods with him, becoming aware of the cycles of life, and observing wildlife in its natural habitat. My father taught me to observe, to be patient, and to apply facts and critical thinking to any situation that I didn't understand. It's not surprising, therefore, that my father's influence drives me to not only communicate with the spirits, but to understand what I'm doing so that I can teach others to do the same.

This interest in science propelled me into presenting my findings and experiences at workshops, symposiums, and conferences with afterlife scientists and researchers in New York, California, and Nevada. A former hospice chaplain and director of the Elisabeth Kübler-Ross Center of Houston is one researcher I came to know and greatly respect. Her name is Dianne Arcangel (for real). She is the author of *Afterlife Encounters* and has amassed a database of 16,500 eyewitness accounts of spirit contact that regular, everyday people have had.

During a weekend conference where we were both speakers, Dianne took the stage first, presenting her research and discussing a current project in which she was exploring the types of personalities most likely to communicate from the other side. At this point I leapt out of my chair and exclaimed, "This is *big* news. The spirits are being tested, not the mediums!" Sometimes my enthusiasm gets the best of me, but I was thrilled that now, studies were extending to the spirit side of the communication equation. After my outburst, which Dianne took in her stride, she continued to present her findings. This research indicated that people with a strong personal presence and creative sensibilities during life on earth were more likely to demonstrate ease in communicating thereafter. For most mediums, this confirms what we already knew, both instinctively and practically. In my experience, more than one event had been dominated by someone in spirit with a strong personal presence who wanted to get their point across . . . again and again.

Following Dianne's lecture, it was my turn to provide an experiential presentation of spirit communication by giving messages from loved ones. Before standing, I asked that those in spirit would use the session as a teaching opportunity, since that was the theme of the conference. After showing the group some hands-on ways to enhance their own connections with spirits, a tiny Asian lady in spirit standing right below the stage caught my eye. Once I acknowledged her, she ran across the front and down one side of the audience, all the way to the back of the auditorium. At first, I thought she was going to run right out the door, but instead, she stopped beside a man sitting in the last row. As she stood there, she gave me the feeling of "mother" and that she was excited about being able to run. When I gave this information to the man in the back, he confirmed that he had an extremely petite mother who had been unable to walk for six years before dying. He used to carry her from room to room. On her deathbed she had told him that she couldn't wait to run again in heaven. As I was speaking with this lovely lady she kept giving me the word "jasmine." When I mentioned this to the man, he had no idea what that meant. She wasn't giving me any more information about it, so I told him that maybe someone else in his family might know what it could mean. It was then time to take a break.

As I was about to continue giving more messages from spirits, the man in the back row stood up. He said, "During the break, I called my sister to see if she would know what 'jasmine' meant. My sister told me that 'jasmine' is the English translation of my mother's Chinese name." There was a hush in the audience as he continued. "When I heard the scientist say that people who are outgoing have an easy time getting through, I thought that I would never hear from my mother. She was a very quiet person and extremely shy." At that point, he choked up and couldn't go on. And that was okay. We were all a little choked up. What this loving mother had showed all of us in that room was that generalizations about spirit communication are not hard-and-fast rules of spirit communication. A mother's love for her son can skew the data. As I was soon to be reminded during the appointments for the day, a son's love for his mother and brother's love for his sister can also reach beyond the boundary of death and skip across the street of skepticism.

Anonymous's Story

I stopped writing this chapter earlier today so that I could work with clients. When I looked at my calendar, one appointment jumped out at me. "Anonymous" was scheduled for a phone session at 11:00 a.m. *Great*, I thought. *Another anonymous.*

As a medium, it is easy to grow weary of the endless "testing" that goes on, especially because it isn't testing in the real sense of the word—it isn't performed in a lab under controlled conditions. A friend once said to me, "You have to prove yourself every day." And while that is true, there is a fallacy inherent in this way of thinking, as spirit communication clearly doesn't depend on a medium's talent alone. As Dianne Arcangel explained, the spirits' abilities to communicate come into play as well. And so does the attitude, belief system, and emotional state of the person receiving the message. Spirit communication is a cooperative effort on the part of all those involved.

My phone rang one minute before the scheduled 11:00 a.m. appointment. "Anonymous" was a woman this time. I began the session like any other, with a prayer. I then had the sense of the spirits surrounding me. Two male spirits, a younger male and an older one, were predominant. The younger male gave me two names, "Jason and Brian." Anonymous said that Jason is the name of the younger male's best friend, but that she didn't know the name "Brian." The young male gave me the start of another name, "Ly." Anonymous said that the young male's brother was named Lyle Brian. She hadn't wanted to acknowledge the name Brian when it came through because it wasn't a first name that she recognized. After a pause, Anonymous said, "I find it interesting that this evidence has come up so early on in the session." The younger male was her son. I was fairly certain that the other male was Anonymous's brother and that was confirmed when he told me that his sense of humor was like a Gary Larson cartoon and that his sister would know exactly what that meant. Anonymous asked, "Did Gary Larson do *The Far Side*? If so, this is interesting because I was ordering a book of *The Far Side* cartoons right before my appointment with you." This is how the session went. The spirits would say something and Anonymous would find it interesting. Brother talked about adoption. Yes, they had been adopted. Brother talked about Anonymous's quest to find her birth mother. He also let me know that he was there with someone who had died by suicide. Yes, her son has passed by suicide. Her son talked about his interest in the science of spirit communication and mentioned that he was reading books with her on the subject. Fortunately, all the information was correct and it actually was interesting.

At the end of our session, I mentioned to Anonymous, who had given me her first name by that time that I was writing about skepticism and science right before our session. "Interesting," was her response. *Interesting indeed*, I thought. I just knew that the irony of it didn't escape her son and her brother. As this experience evidences, sometimes my life is more about living on the far side than communicating with the other side.

Opening up the Floodgates

Several years ago, I was asked to speak at an event sponsored by an organization supporting people who had suffered the loss of a child. After being introduced, I walked out in front of the crowd. I was silent and so too was the crowd. I was struck by two things immediately: the palpable, dense energy of grief that rolled toward me nearly knocking me off my feet and the fact that I couldn't see any spirits among all the faces.

I reminded myself to breathe. "Come on," I said to whoever in spirit might be listening. "We can't disappoint these people." It was then that I became aware of a group encircling the room. There were kids of all ages lining up against the wall. There were so many spirits, in fact, that most of their outlines were indistinct. I looked at them. They looked at me. Silently.

I've been asked if I ever get scared doing this work. Yes, I do, but only when the spirits don't speak to me. This was one of those scary times.

I really didn't know what to do. These kids weren't playing by my rules.

I scanned the crowd once again and saw an elderly gentleman in spirit standing behind a man in the audience. *Whew,* I thought. *At least we can get started.* The gentleman in spirit identified himself as the father of the man sitting before me. He provided information about himself and the family. In my mind's eye he showed me a photo of himself holding a baby in his arms and he gave me the name, Jenny. The man in the audience confirmed that he did indeed have a photo of his father holding his daughter, Jenny, in his arms shortly after she had been born. The gentleman in spirit then went on to say, "I want you to know that I am still holding Jenny in my arms. You thought she died because you had failed to protect her." The man in the audience couldn't seem to catch his breath. He finally replied, "When Jenny died, I asked my father to take care of her in heaven." He seemed to be struggling with his next words, which were, "Because I couldn't protect her."

Messages during the entire evening were similar. Devastated parents were comforted by parents and relatives in spirit, even though the kids in spirit still surrounded the room in silence. The grief of the parents sitting in front of me began to feel less forceful, but it still felt solid. In my mind, I had a vision of a dike holding back water wanting to rush in all over us. There were holes in the dike, but it still held. At that moment, I didn't understand what I was seeing.

At the end of the night, I left exhausted. Like the father who had thought he had failed at protecting his daughter, I felt as though I had failed to connect parents with their beloved children in spirit.

The next morning during my prayer and meditation time, I cried. "What happened?" I asked my helper spirits. "How can I serve the spirits better?"

The answer I received came in two ways. The first was a vision in which I saw the same dike that I had seen the night before. The dike was intact at first, then water began leaking through some holes that had formed from sheer pressure. After a while the mounting force was so great that the water pounded through the dike, rushing toward me with crushing speed and intensity. It was a terrifying vision, but it got my attention. And yet, I still didn't fully comprehend it. So I sat and waited. When the answer came, it was in a flash.

When someone we love dies, it feels as though death has created an impenetrable wall or dike that separates us from everyone, everything, and even life itself. However it isn't death that creates this wall, nor is the wall so solid that it can't be permeated by those in spirit. It is our feelings of loss, anger, failure, and guilt around someone's passing that add piles of dirt to the dike, making it appear even thicker than it actually is. Yes, losing someone we love causes suffering. What we believe about the way they died also adds to that suffering, until it becomes so difficult, and sometimes almost impossible, for the spirits to break through. But it doesn't have to be that way.

Sometimes a singular spirit communication can poke holes in our dikes of grief; other times the cumulative effect of a number of little holes is needed to break down the dike so that the spirits can flood us with their love; and of course, there are those times when the dike stands firm for a long, long time.

Next, my helpers showed me an image of all the kids the night before, standing around the perimeter of the room. "They *chose* to stand as a group against the wall," my helpers said. "They knew that if one or a few of them spoke to their parents, the others would feel that their own children didn't love them enough to come." Instead, they allowed messages from the grandparents to start the process of poking holes in the dike so that in time the love of the children could come pouring through.

For a moment, I considered the wisdom of those kids. Kids in spirit are willing to play the game of love in unexpected ways because they know that in the end, they'll win.

Spirit ANSWERS

When you're working as a medium, do you actually see the spirits? Do you hear them speaking to you?

When I was young, and also when I first started as a professional medium, the spirits I saw were very clear, very real. I could have described them completely head to toe. After years of doing the work, my guides and the spirits have developed a shorthand way for me to connect specifically with the loved ones of people who come to see me. Part of the reason for this, I think, is that they've figured out how to use energy efficiently and effectively to communicate distinguishing characteristics while also preserving my energy for my own well-being.

Here's an example of how the spirits work with me these days: At a group event in Maryland, a young woman in spirit showed me a picture in my mind of beautiful blue eyes, a perfect smile . . . and a trophy. I didn't see her entire face. When I mentioned this image to her mother, I was told that her daughter had won a trophy in high school for having the most beautiful eyes and smile in the school. In this instance I was shown only what was important for the sake of identifying this young woman in spirit.

During events, my physical eye may be caught by a movement or an impression of a spirit standing near a person or group. Rather than the spirits fully manifesting beside their loved ones, they use what I call "the movie screen of my mind" to project images and symbols that are significant points of identification. In some situations, I may actually see a vision—similar to a short film. When I see a vision, I really pay attention to it because, for me, visions often represent a bigger concept regarding life here and in the afterlife.

Spirits like to use symbol shorthand with me to provide information about themselves and their loved ones. Some of these symbols include stop signs, the international "no" symbol, and an upraised mug (signifying alcohol consumption). For example, during a session with a woman and her mother in spirit, the symbol for house (which looks like a little plastic Monopoly piece) appeared over the woman's head. This is the shorthand for "you're buying a house or have just bought a house." When a spirit shows me a bunch of these little Monopoly houses over a sitter's head, it often means that person is in the real estate business.

I couldn't begin to list the entire lexicon of symbols that the spirits use with me. In some of the accounts in this book, you may notice how a spirit will use symbols to communicate a concept or message.

I'm convinced that the spirits will use a medium's interests and background to get their points across as well. For example, my grandmother, my mother, and I love books, words, crossword puzzles, and the like. When spirits communicate with me, I sometimes experience what I call spirit skywriting, which is when words seem to be written or drawn before my eyes. Another love of mine is music, so the spirits may drop song titles into my head or I'll hear a song playing in my inner ear as though I've got an iPod imbedded there.

Part of my job as a medium is to take the symbols, visions, spirit skywriting, songs—all the bits of information provided by the spirits—and put it together into a whole picture that is recognizable to the people who so desperately want to connect.

In answering the question about hearing spirit voices, I would say that, yes, I have heard spirit voices *in the air*. This is a very rare occurrence, and I think I can remember each time it has happened. One of those times is recounted in this book. On the whole, the spirits speak to me in another way entirely, which I call hearing with the "inner ear."

You can think of it this way: Most of us have an inner dialogue running most of the day. We can converse with friends and family, and all the while there is an inner voice commenting on what's happening. I am able to quiet my own inner dialogue and allow the spirits to use that mechanism to be heard. When I "hear" the spirits say something, it can be anything from a name to a few words and even an entire phrase or sentence. For instance, I may hear a name or part of a name in my inner ear. If the spirit isn't getting through with an entire name, I might hear something that sounds like "Ch-ch-ch"—for example, if a spirit is trying to convey the name "Charlie."

There are times, however, when a spirit is particularly adept at using my mind, and whole phrases and sentences are dropped *entirely* into my head. Sometimes these thoughts arrive so suddenly and with such force that it sounds like shouting in my head. In these exceptional cases (many of which are shared in this book), I am struck by how "not me" the messages are and how meaningful they could be for many people. I treasure those moments of stunning clarity and work toward making myself available for more and more of them.

Can mediums turn on and off communications with spirits like they do a radio?

Thankfully, yes. If this weren't the case, mediums wouldn't be able to go to the grocery store, raise their own families, or go to the movies without a constant barrage of spirits. After all, spirits are around us all the time.

The radio analogy is a good one. We're surrounded by radio waves but the only time the music is heard is when a receiver is tuned to a certain frequency. It's the same way with mediums. For instance, when I'm tackling my daily to-do list, my brain is tuned to the earth's radio station. When it is time to connect with spirits, my brain's waves shift and I become a receiver for the spirits' radio station. These different states of consciousness (or tuning in) are practical only when used at the right time. When I'm tuned in to the spirits, my ability to function in the everyday world is extremely diminished. I'm in a state that I call "fuzzy-brained." (Some might say that this is my usual state, but they're wrong!) When in the "fuzzy-brained" state, it is difficult to drive and perform any task that requires cognition. I can become extremely disoriented. So when I'm in the grocery store picking out cabbage for my perfect slaw, I tune in to the earth station so that I'm not distracted by all the spirits roaming around in the produce section and come home with kale instead. (Don't laugh, it's been known to happen!) When it is time, however, to communicate with the spirits, I tune out my everyday consciousness (the bill paying, etc.) and tune in to the spirits' radio station (my "fuzzy-brain" state) so that I can hear the music of their voices.

Do mediums hear the dead in their sleep, or only when they are awake?

It is actually even easier to connect with the spirit world while sleeping—not just for mediums, but for everyone! When we're asleep, and the concerns of the physical are not demanding our attention, we are simply more receptive to experiences beyond ourselves and the limitations of our world. While I was growing up, as I mentioned earlier, nighttime was *the* time for spirit activity in my house. Before I went to sleep, in my dreams, and in the time just before waking up entirely, there were spirits around me—some wanting to interact and others just milling about. These days, with very few exceptions, the time and place for spirit interactions is planned and I can turn my receptivity on when needed and turn it off when it is time to rest. I'll share more about connecting with loved ones in spirit through dreams in the chapter called, "Bringing Heaven Home."

Do mediums have conversations with spirits or are they just expected to be good listeners?

One of the things I enjoy most about spirit communication is that it is *interactive*. Although not entirely conversational, there is a back-and-forth that goes on in thought between the medium and those in spirit. When I'm in a session with a sitter, I ask that the spirits provide me with information that identifies them specifically. Once their identity is established, I am open to receiving messages for the sitter. After all, a message only has value if we know its source. Here's an example of a conversation with a spirit: during a phone session, Boomer, a young man in spirit, provided details about himself (his name, favorite hobbies, his love for the beach), his life (where he had gone to school, the car parts still sitting in the garage), his family (a younger sister that he was still protecting and a dad who was suffering tremendously because of his death), and the new therapy dog that his mother was training. He then told me that he had a lady with him who had committed suicide. His mother, on the other end of the phone, responded sharply with, "No one in my family has committed suicide. I have *no* idea what that means." In my mind I said to Boomer, "She doesn't get it. Can you give me anything else that will help?" At that moment, the name, Ritchie, popped into my head. I said to his mother, "Your son gave me the name Ritchie." She gasped and said, "Ritchie is my son's best friend and Ritchie's mother killed herself two weeks ago." Boomer's mother then told me that after hearing about Ritchie's mom, she had been wondering if her son knew of his friend's loss. However, if I had only been in listening mode during this session, Boomer's mother and I might have missed the answer to the question she had actually been asking days *before* the session even began. Boomer had heard his mother's question, "Boomer, do you know about Richie's mom?" and was ready with an answer. Continuing conversations through a medium is one more way a loved one in spirit lets those still here know that they're listening. Hints for having your own "conversations" with spirits are explained in the appendix, "Is Anybody There?"

Is there a reason why I'm the only one in my family who sees my relatives in spirit?

Being the only one to see relatives in spirit doesn't mean that they loved you best (although it might be nice to think so). There are a number of reasons why this may be true, so let's start with the most common.

First of all, you may have psychic talent and sensitivity to spirits whether you realize it or not. Sometimes a tragedy is the activating force that jump-starts the awareness of our own abilities. This activation may happen immediately, in which case you may experience visitations in dreams or a myriad of other ways thereafter. Or activation may happen over time and with some determination on your part. Vivian, a woman I met while teaching a workshop, is an example of this kind of determination. Vivian's daughter, Paige, died at the age of seventeen after a long struggle with an illness. Vivian, who desperately wanted to know that Paige was okay, started reading everything she could about spirit communication. All this reading inspired her to consider that spirit communication was possible. She then attended demonstrations of mediumship, which convinced her that it was real. For her next step, she went on retreats and attended workshops to further develop awareness. Ultimately this gave her the tools to be open to spirits herself. Now after years of practice, Vivian is not only aware of her daughter, Paige, but is able to provide messages to others who have lost loved ones too.

Secondly, there may be those within the family whose grief runs so deep that they cannot be open to someone in spirit as much as they may want to be. Their systems are so overloaded with emotion that it is impossible for the subtle energy of those in spirit to be felt. In these circumstances, spirits may pop in and visit other relatives (aunts, cousins, or even second cousins) for whom the loss doesn't create the same sense of alienation from life. *You* might be that person. An example of this came up at a group event in Maryland. When I looked out into the audience, I saw a young man in spirit (he looked to be about fifteen), standing behind one woman, with his hand resting on the shoulder of the lady next to her. At first I thought that I was seeing double—these ladies looked almost identical! Fortunately, they were dressed differently and each styled her hair differently as well. This young man gave me the sense that the woman he was standing behind was his mother. He gave me the name "Jeffrey" and held up a baseball, and at that moment I had the sensation of a sudden impact at my right temple. When I passed along this information to his mother, she started to cry and couldn't speak. The lady next to her confirmed that Jeffrey had died after being hit in the head with a baseball. Jeffrey gave me the thought that he had been visiting the lady who was speaking to me, but that she was afraid to tell anyone about it. She confirmed this by saying, "Yes. Jeffrey is my nephew. After he died, he started to visit me in my dreams and then I thought I saw him in my den when my husband was watching a baseball game. I was afraid to tell anyone because my sister so desperately wanted to see her son and yet he was coming to me! I thought that maybe because his mother and I are twins, he got confused and came to the wrong house!" I asked Jeffrey why he was coming to his aunt and not his mother and he conveyed the thought, "It's easier." Jeffrey's right. Sometimes it is just easier to get a message through to someone who is close, but not the closest.

Another reason why you may be the only one in the family seeing a relative in spirit is because that person desires to heal a personal connection with you that was broken by distance, misunderstanding, judgment and/or death. I'm reminded of a situation with three sisters who came for a sitting a number of years ago. As they sat down together, I glimpsed a lady in spirit with perfectly coiffed hair and lots of jewelry standing behind one of the sisters. The spirit gave me the feeling of a mother bond. Then I felt suddenly exhausted as though the life was draining right out of me. This is often the feeling I get in the presence of a spirit who has passed with cancer. The mother then dropped the thought into my head that the daughter she was standing behind was able to see her. When I passed along all that information, the three girls said (practically in unison), "That's why we're here." Their mother went on to say that she appreciated the love, care, and attention that two of the three girls had given her when she was dying of cancer. She thanked them for allowing her to die in her own home with dignity. "We shared so many special memories together," their mother told me. She was then emphatic (as emphatic as a spirit gets with me) when she said to the third daughter, "I come to visit you because you weren't with your sisters and me when I was sick. I want you to know that I love you and am happy that you and your sisters are together again." At this point, the ladies started crying and we passed the tissues around. The "prodigal sister" confirmed that she couldn't handle being around the family as her mother was dying; she had always felt misunderstood and like an outsider in her own family. The other two sisters, although glad that they were finally reunited with the third sister, were a bit put out that she had been the only one to have seen their mother in spirit. Because their mother did something unexpected, however, it prompted all of them to come together to figure things out.

And finally, you may also be the only person in your family to see loved ones in spirit because that's your job. Just as there may be a great cook in your family or a wonderful storyteller or singer, your function may be what I call "designated healer." This person is often sensitive and has an inner desire to be a peacemaker and healer, not just within the family, but in the wider world as well. Their families may face serious challenges like abuse and addictions of all sorts. While a designated healer has tremendous empathy for people and may frequently want to fix things to make everything okay for all those around them, they can sometimes do so at great emotional, physical, and financial cost. However, if a designated healer starts establishing clear boundaries while working more with those in spirit, "healing" can take the place of "fixing."

Will spirits let me know when I'm going to die?

No need to worry about that. One of the laws of spirit interaction is that spirits cannot interfere with either our destiny or our free will unless we give them permission to do so or we abdicate our personal responsibility. Spirits can guide, they can support, they can inspire, and they can warn, but they do not cause or predict someone's passing.

That being said, those who are close to passing may talk to spirits that others cannot see. It is common for people who are near dying to see loved ones who have passed before them and to converse with them, sometimes laughing as though sharing a private cosmic joke. Oftentimes, these conversations with those unseen loved ones are presumed to be the result of pain medication or dementia. During sessions, however, loved ones in spirit will often mention who showed up to help them make the transition from life through death and into new life.

There are also spirits on the other side whose job is to help as the time of death nears. These spirits aren't necessarily friends and relatives, but they can help prepare people for the transition and escort them to heaven. For instance, when my mother was coming toward the end of her struggle with multiple myeloma, she was more animated one morning than usual. When I entered her hospital room, she couldn't wait to tell me about all the Chinese children who had come to visit her during the night. "They were so adorable in their little school outfits," she told me. "There was an entire class and they brought pretty pictures to show me." I listened to her news with what I hoped seemed like enthusiasm, all the while making a note to request a change in her medication. Later on that evening, though, I came to a different conclusion. I'm a medium after all, so I thought I should at least consider that my mother could see spirits, too. As I sat contemplating what she had told me, I was struck by how appropriate it was that a group of school children from a foreign country would come and cheer up my mom. My mother had dedicated her life to teaching young children and she was fascinated by world cultures. "Remember, Holli," she used to say to me, "you are a citizen of the United States but you are also a citizen of the world." So instead of doubting my mother's experience, I thanked those children for bringing delight and joy to her during the days of illness when any relief from pain and despair was a blessing.

Spirit SUMMARY

Loved ones in spirit desire to reconnect with us, maybe even *more* than we want to hear from them. However, if grief is especially dense, it can create a barrier between this world and the next. Despite challenges, the spirits teach us that where there is love, there is a way to connect. This is especially true with kids in spirit. They break through grief and circumvent blocks of skepticism by using creative ways to get their messages across. As a medium, I'm often amazed at the determination of kids to touch their parents and friends with their love from the afterlife.

3

Oops!

What Kids Say about Dying by Accident

Spirit TWEET

"The last thing I saw was the light; the first thing I saw was the light." (Said by a young man who crashed into a light pole while skateboarding and died instantly.)

Spirit THOUGHTS

A Hitchhiker's Guide to Life

It was an early spring day with the memory of winter still crisp in the air. The peaks of the eastern Sierras dwarfed my small car as I sped toward a famed ski resort for a series of scheduled events and sessions. The temperature dropped as the altitude rose. I anxiously watched the clock and *not* the speedometer because I had gotten a late start leaving Los Angeles. Then out of the corner of my eye, I saw him.

Alongside the road just outside the mountain town, a young man walked casually with what looked like a snowboard hanging off his right shoulder. I returned my eyes to the road. And then, I felt him. He and his board were sitting in the passenger's seat. I sighed. It wasn't the first time that I had picked up a spirit hitchhiker on this particular road.

When I first traveled to the area, a pioneer woman named Elizabeth appeared in my car. As soon as I arrived at my first group event, I mentioned that Elizabeth had guided my covered wagon (which is what she called my ragtop) to the destination. The husband of the lady who had arranged the event turned pale and then told us that his great grandmother was named Elizabeth and had come to the area in a covered wagon. This man, who had been humoring his wife with all this "spirit stuff," has since become a dear friend.

On another trip to this same area, a young man in spirit who had lived on the reservation hopped into my car. He let me know that he had died from a gunshot wound, although I didn't see a scratch on him. When I mentioned this at the first event, several people knew of the shooting and one lady's daughter had been his best friend in high school. This young man had been shot because a drunken man mistook him for someone else. He died of his wounds two weeks before high school graduation.

Another time, a trooper who had been killed in the line of duty told me to slow down. Of course I was speeding . . . again. (When someone in spirit tells you to slow down, you listen.)

I don't pick up hitchhikers as a rule. But for some reason, they always stick their thumbs out along this particular highway.

So I didn't think much about it when this young man with the board decided to catch a ride. However, after reaching my hotel and checking in, I could still feel him with me. He was quite the attentive welcoming committee.

Within an hour of arriving, I was at a small event. As I scanned the group, this same young man paced impatiently until the introduction and opening prayer were finished. He then came to stand behind a beautiful young woman named Bailey, who had come to the event with her mother.

I described the young man to Bailey, his long, dirty blond hair, his killer smile, his ice-blue eyes. I also told her that he met me on the highway right outside of town and was carrying a board (which I assumed to be a snowboard). He gave me two names, his own, Jerry, and that of a friend, Paul. Bailey's eyes grew wide. Paul was a friend of *hers*. He then gave me the word "teacher" and glanced over to Bailey's mother. Bailey's mother exclaimed, "I know this boy! He was one of my students." Jerry went on to describe his memorial service, which Bailey's mother had attended. It seemed strange to me that Jerry wasn't here to speak with a parent or other relative, but with a young woman with whom he only shared a mutual friend. However, after working with those in spirit for so many years, I knew that there would be a reason . . . and a good one.

Jerry then went on to say, "I died doing what I love" and held up his board. Bailey knew exactly what he was talking about. Jerry had died in a skateboarding accident during an exhibition in Japan. (I hadn't seen wheels on his board and assumed that it was a snowboard.) This young man had such an artistic way about him. He was gentle, kind, and very funny. He let me know that Bailey had stopped college because she was struggling with choices in life. She wanted to be a graphic artist, but thought that she wasn't good enough. Bailey understood everything that Jerry said. He told me that she had asked for guidance that night and he was sent to talk to her. His parting advice was "Don't be afraid to do what you love. Just do it." And then, like a Nike swoosh, he was gone.

After a moment of silence, Bailey said, "Before coming here tonight, I asked to hear from a guide—and I wanted him to be cute!" Of course, we all laughed.

Jerry was indeed cute, but more than that, he was smart, funny . . . and wise.

That night before going to bed, I thought about the visit from Jerry. Sometimes, I find what those in spirit don't say just as interesting as what they do say. Not once during Jerry's time with me did he give me the feeling of being disappointed that he hadn't lived longer. Not once did he blame himself or someone else for his death. Not once did it seem strange to him that he was reaching out beyond his closest relationships. He didn't mention one "if only" as in, "If only I hadn't gone on that trip," or, "If only I had worn a helmet," or, "If only I hadn't taken that jump." His advice to Bailey wasn't to live a safe or limited life. His advice was to live a life of self expression. Just do it.

As I've mentioned before, young people in spirit often shy away from dwelling on their death and dying experiences. However, those they've left behind often imagine that their loved one's death was scary and painful and could have been avoided. In these cases, kids often go out of their way to set the record straight. When one mother sat before me, her son in spirit kept repeating over and over that he hadn't been scared. He wanted her to know that his was an *instant* transition. But this grieving mother couldn't get away from the idea that if someone had been with her son right after his accident, he could have been saved. She imagined that he had lingered, terrified, while dying alone. Up to this point in the session, her son hadn't told me how he had passed. All I could hear was the sound of a skateboard on pavement. He showed me a snapshot of a skateboard and a streetlight in my mind. He gave me no sense of fear. No pain. Then he said, "The last thing I saw was the light; the first thing I saw was the light." It was only then that his mother told me that while skateboarding, he had crashed into a light pole and was found crumpled and dead at its base. In these few poetic words, he summed up his instantaneous death and birth into the afterlife while putting his mother's horrifying speculations to rest.

No-Fault Assurances

When I first started working as a medium, I didn't want to face children in spirit. In my prayers I'd say, "Use my talents in every way *except* talking to kids." Actually, what I couldn't face was feeling the pain of parents in grief. Frankly, even the thought terrified me. So what did the spirits do in response to my plea? They sent me three groups of grieving parents and grandparents in *one* week. Those in spirit wouldn't let my personal fear interfere with *their* plans.

Sioban entered my office, sat down quietly, clasped her hands, and refused to look at me. Her beloved grandmother in spirit came to visit. Her grandmother, Nana, gave me the feeling of a stroke (which was how she died), and I smelled the fish dish for which she was famous. Nana gave me the feeling that she hadn't come alone. I heard the name, "Jackie." At the mention of "Jackie," Sioban's shoulders stiffened and she brought her hands to her eyes. And then I was shown a car seat with a tan-, blue-, and white-striped cushion and a black SUV. I heard, "Mommy, I'm okay. I'm with Nana." When I passed the message along, Sioban started to sob. "Please help me," I pleaded to my spirit helpers. As I looked toward Sioban, I saw a little spirit boy who was about three years old trying to crawl up into her lap. "Mommy, I know you didn't mean it," little Jackie said. I told Sioban that Jackie knew she didn't mean it. (I still didn't know what "it" was.) In that moment, an immense and powerful tsunami of love came flooding over and through me from Jackie for Sioban. I almost forgot to breathe. All I could say was, "Jackie loves you."

After those words, Sioban looked into my eyes for the first time. She said two words, "Thank you." As I was walking with her to the front door, Sioban told me that one day while backing her SUV out of the garage, she hadn't seen Jackie behind the vehicle. By accident, she had hit her own son. (This incident occurred before extensive rearview monitors were installed in larger vehicles.) Since that day, she hadn't been able to drive the SUV that was still sitting in the driveway with her son's car seat inside, the one with the striped cushion. Just before turning to walk away, Sioban said, "I thought my son hated me for what I did to him. If he can still love me, maybe someday I'll stop blaming myself."

The other sessions with parents that I had that same week were similar. All the children had died accidentally either due to an action by a relative or with a parent present. All of the children expressed tremendous love for their parents despite the way that they had died. All of the parents blamed themselves. None of the children blamed their parents.

In and around metaphysical circles I've heard people say,

"There's no such thing as an accident." I've also heard people say, "You die when it is your time to go." I've even heard people say that God wanted a child back. *Could God be so cruel as to take a child away from parents? Could any of these statements be true even in cases when children die accidentally at the hands of their own parents?* I needed answers. I needed to understand.

When I ask a question, those in spirit often respond with experiences rather than fast and easy answers. Some answers have come through accidents I've experienced myself including a car accident, an accidental fall at work, and another accident wherein I was whisked away by a rip current off the coast of San Diego. Other answers have come from speaking with innumerable young people who died what we would call "accidental deaths." Through all of these experiences, I've begun to understand "accidents" from the points of view of kids in heaven.

From our perspective, an accident can be viewed as a tragic coincidence at best, or at worst, as a way that those left behind pay for real or perceived failures. Kids in spirit, however, see accidents as opportunities. They see accidents as a chance to experience and understand physical limits, provoke forgiveness, and effect change.

First of all, kids on earth learn more about the limits of the physical world through interacting with it than by listening to the experiences of others. When they first begin to walk, they learn about gravity by falling. When they first begin to drive, they discover the power of speed. They also attempt to text, fix their hair, eat chips, and sing along with their favorite songs, all while driving in traffic. Testing physical boundaries is a primary interest of kids on earth—and from heaven.

A young aspiring musician in spirit came to speak with his

mother and sister during a session on his birthday. He explained that they weren't with him when he passed. He was sensitive and very serious in his demeanor. He described his custom guitar, his digs by the beach, his plan to record his music, and his love affair . . . with heroin. This boy saw heroin as his muse, his inspiration. He showed me a picture in my mind of his bedroom and on the bedside table was a book. He told me that he had read about how to use heroin to juice his creativity *without* becoming addicted. His mother and sister confirmed and understood everything that he was communicating to me. That book about using heroin had been found by his sister on the bedside table next to his body. This young man had died of an accidental overdose. His mother said to him in my presence, "We all tried to warn you, but you wouldn't listen." His sister asked him, "What was your first thought when you found out that *we* were right?" He answered, "Oops!" This was probably not the answer that she was expecting. She retorted right back as a sister would. "Yeah, *big* oops," she said.

When referring to their own deaths, I have *never* had a young person in heaven tell me that it was just their time to go. Living life by the clock is foreign to kids when they first arrive here on earth. Babies cry when they're hungry but learn by a later age that dinner is at 6:00 p.m. Kids don't project into the future, they live in the moment. And that is the way they live in heaven, too.

Jesse's Road Home

During a group session, Jesse, a teen in spirit, talked about his pride in learning how to drive. He was a good driver, he insisted on telling me. "Yes, he was," his mother replied. "That's why they were surprised by the way I died," he told me. He showed me an image of himself in spirit watching as his mother drove back and forth along a deserted country road. He was trying to catch her attention to let her know that he was okay. Not only couldn't she see him in his spirit body, but she didn't see his car buried deep in a ravine. While driving home after work, he had taken a curve too fast and ran off the road. "How can I go on living without him?" Jesse's mom asked. Instead, Jesse became much younger before my eyes and started jumping up and down. He placed Mickey Mouse ears on his head, which is my symbol for a vacation at Disneyland or Disney World. His mom started to laugh through her tears. She remembered that when the family had been chosen to ride a float in a Disney World parade, the only member of the family jumping up and down and waving arms was her son. He wasn't doing a dance because he had been instructed to do so. Rather, he was jumping out of sheer joy. In that moment of joy, he inspired the entire family, even his father, to jump up and down and dance with hula hoops. This boy who died as a teenager was still the child who danced at Disney World. His experiences in life and death exist at the same time in heaven. And he believed that the joy he experienced with his family at Disney World was still as available to them as it was to him. He didn't see the joy of that experience as being in the past, but in the present. Kids in spirit live in the present tense.

When an accident results in a loved one's death, there's always the impulse to blame someone else or ourselves. There must have been something that could have been done, we reason. If there isn't someone to blame on earth, then we can blame God for claiming what was ours. Kids in spirit, however, don't blame and they don't hold grudges. They see accidents as opportunities for forgiveness.

Lisa's View from the Mountain

In a town surrounded by mountains, I met a girl in spirit who demonstrated the power of forgiveness. At the start of an event I was participating in, I could feel a spirit standing next to me. She had long blond hair and was tall and willowy, like a dancer. I heard the words *Lisa* and *daughter* as thoughts in my head. As I described my impressions of who was standing next to me, a woman named Roberta told me that Lisa was her daughter. Lisa showed me pictures of her doll collection sitting on a shelf in her room. She talked about dancing, about her boyfriend, Bart, and her first semester at college.

Then Lisa did something unexpected. She *wanted* to share her death with me. She started projecting a movie onto a blank screen right in front of my eyes. On a dark mountain road, a car wound its way around the curves. Then out of nowhere, a truck appeared. I felt struck and pushed. No fear. No pain. Roberta confirmed that her daughter had died when her car was hit by a truck as she was driving home from school.

I was surprised that Lisa had decided to be so cinematic in describing her death. Then she told me why. Lisa explained by putting thoughts in my mind that the truck driver had been suffering greatly since her death. He needed to know that she didn't blame him. He needed to hear that he was forgiven.

Roberta knew who the truck driver was. She even had contact information for him.

Weeks later, I was informed that Roberta had called the truck driver's home. In speaking with his wife, she learned that he had not driven a truck since the day her daughter died. His life since the accident had been a living hell. His wife said that he hadn't had a good night's sleep since then and was reliving the accident again and again. Roberta shared the conversation she had had with her daughter in spirit and asked that the truck driver's wife pass along the message that he was forgiven. Lisa's message of forgiveness helped start the healing process for three people: her mother, the truck driver, and his wife.

Kids in spirit don't play the role of victim when they come to me. Instead, they seem interested in creating change in the world even though they're no longer physically *in* the world. Kids in heaven join their families in causes that may have been inspired by their lives and create positive legacies that survive their passing.

Michael's Bike-a-thon for Safety

At a small group event, a nine-year-old boy in spirit holding a balloon and proudly displaying a red bike stood by a woman who was nodding enthusiastically as others received their messages. This young boy in spirit seemed happy to wait his turn, which is unusual for young boys. When I told this woman that a polite boy was standing next to her, she acknowledged that she had a son in spirit who was *very* polite and patient. The red bike was important, she told me, and so was the balloon. She asked me if her son had been with her and his father the day before. When I silently asked her son the question, he showed me bikes, bike helmets, lots of balloons, and his parents in the middle of a crowd. When I shared this scene with his mother, she told me that they had been distributing helmets to needy children who were bike riders. To sweeten the pot, they also handed out balloons. The money for the helmets was raised in her son's memory. He had died after falling off his bicycle because he hadn't been wearing a helmet. When she and her husband brought a balloon home from the event, it danced around the living room and then seemed to follow her from room to room. After finding no drafts, she thought that it might have been her son letting her know that he was around.

During sessions and events, many young people in spirit have mentioned that trees have been planted in their honor, scholarship funds started in their names and foundations and charities created by their families. Wherever there is the opportunity for positive change, kids in spirit are there.

This is not to say that every family that has a child die is going to form a foundation, a scholarship fund, or a charity. Nor is this a suggestion that every family must. Kids will participate in *any* growth and change, even if it is a change of heart by one person in silent prayer. *Wherever* there is the opportunity for positive change, kids in spirit are there. Kids grow and change. That's what they do here on earth . . . and that's what they help us to do from the afterlife.

Kids use what seems accidental as an opportunity to bring even more love into the world. And *that's* no accident.

Spirit ANSWERS

Is there a difference between a psychic and a medium?

Although often assumed to be the same, there are significant differences between the work of psychics and mediums. The primary difference is that the source of their input is different. Psychics interpret information from the energy around people, places, and things here on the earth. Mediums, on the other hand, relay information, and specific details received from a distinct, recognizable person in spirit. The ways in which psychics and mediums receive and process the information can be very similar, which can add to the confusion. Both, for instance, may be skilled in clairvoyance, which means literally "to see clearly," and clairaudience, which means literally "to hear clearly." It's easy to think of it this way: psychics and mediums are like computers in that they both process information. Their operating system is the same, but their servers are different. Psychics are connected to the earth's server and mediums are connected not only to the earth's server, but to the spirits' server as well.

To help further clarify the functional difference between psychics and mediums, here's an example:

Let's say that you were in the process of interviewing for a great job and you wanted some advice about the situation. On the way to see a psychic, you're thinking, "I really, really, *really* want that job!" Well, when you walk into the psychic's office, she looks at you and says, "You really want a job!" And you think, "Wow, she's good." Because your thoughts and intentions imprint the energy field around you (what is called your "aura"), the psychic can pick up on those imprints. A psychic might then receive impressions about the person who interviewed you and see pictures of the company's offices in her mind. Psychics can usually follow the energy set by your interaction with the person to see if it is leading toward receiving the job.

If you choose to see a medium instead, the medium might say something like, "I have a man here in spirit who comes in as a father, or father figure. He's a tall man. He gives me pain in my chest like a heart attack and a name that starts with *L* and sounds like "Lou." This Lou was a hardworking man and gives me the idea that you're interested in getting a job." At this point, Lou may provide insights about your work life in general or this particular job, but from his own individual perspective. Those in spirit prefer to provide guidance rather than predict the future. One of the reasons for this is that loved ones in spirit respect our freedom to choose; they honor our free will.

When you die, is it just your time to go?

We aren't born with an egg timer inside of us that dings when we're done. We do, however, enter this world with a destiny, a checklist, and contracts to fulfill along with the free will required to make decisions. All of this is wrapped up in our body, a living, fragile spirit container.

It might be easier if you think of it this way. Our overall destiny includes the gifts and talents we bring with us to make a difference in this world. There are those who will be inspiring spiritual teachers, talented entertainers, or brilliant scientists. A soul's checklist is the wish list for our life on earth. The checklist might contain things like "I need a dose of compassion this time around," or "I need to learn to be responsible where money is concerned." Our contracts often include unfinished business with those who incarnate with us (friends, families, and even strangers with whom you feel connected). Contracts can be agreements and vows we've made with ourselves before coming to the earth, or vows we make once we're here. For example, when people enter a religious order, they take vows of poverty or chastity. We do the same thing almost every day when we make statements like, "I'll never do *that* again." It is important to remember that these contracts and vows remain in effect until revoked or changed.

Fortunately, we have free will to handle what might seem like a complicated mix in our lives. Free will gives us the ability to choose to become more conscious and aware of our checklists, agendas, and contracts and change them when we choose. Some people come into this world with expansive agendas or destinies but very few checklists. Our world's greatest spiritual leaders seem to fall into that category. Other people enter the world with huge checklists and contracts. People like this seem to always have a lot to deal with in their lives and may have much to overcome. Others choose to wrap up their checklists and agendas and fulfill their contracts at lightning speed and may not live long lives. When and how we die isn't as much a question of timing as it is a junction of the four directions of destiny, contracts, checklists, and free will.

Is heaven really like a giant Neverland?

Well, if you mean that when we get to heaven we never have to grow up, that's not what spirits tell me. Life in the afterlife provides an opportunity to take an unflinching look at the way we lived life on earth. Depending on choices we've made, this may or may not be entirely pleasant. A man who drank himself to death told me, "Dying was a sobering experience." For him, I'm sure it was.

Every spirit I meet tells me what his or her heaven is like. Although there are common themes in these communications, contrasting and sometimes contradictory details are provided as well. As a medium, I know that I am only given glimpses of what exists beyond our life on earth. Despite the variety of perspectives I've received from the spirits, I couldn't begin to describe the afterlife fully and completely.

When I get together with friends who are mediums, there are often lively debates about life, death, and the afterlife. To use a much-worn analogy, mediums are like blind men trying to describe an elephant. When one touches the trunk, he says that the elephant is like a snake. Describing heaven is a lot like that. The afterlife is so immense and so beyond our human understanding that different descriptions may be valid, even if they seem contradictory.

Does forgiving someone who has done something wrong just let them off the hook too easily?

When someone hurts you or someone you love, it is natural to want to make it right, and teach someone a lesson in the bargain. It is easy to think that by *not* forgiving someone, their lives will be adversely affected. However, the very opposite is true. I like to think of it this way: although it is natural for a fish to grab the bait at the end of the hook, he quickly learns that once the hook is set, he can no longer swim in the direction he chooses; his freedom and his life are now controlled by someone else. When we take the bait of anger, judgment, and resentment, we're the ones on the hook, not the person who did us wrong. However, by willing to forgive someone's actions or our own, the hook is removed and we can swim freely once again. When you forgive someone, the only person getting off the hook is *you*.

Do spirits have roles or responsibilities in heaven?

Many spirits, including guides and angels, populate the unseen world. Most spirits do have roles and responsibilities. Guides, for instance, help us to stay on course during our journey on earth. The "helper spirits" I work with keep the spirit communication process organized. The primary purpose of my work is to connect people on earth with their relatives and friends living in spirit and they, too, have mentioned working in the afterlife. However, their interest is usually directed toward helping those they've left behind on earth. Many spirits have told me that it is only by dying that they have accepted full responsibility for their actions on earth. Ironically enough, taking responsibility for what has been done already seems to be even more important than taking on new heavenly responsibilities.

How do spirits spend their time?

Thankfully, there are no clocks in the afterlife and time as we know it doesn't affect the spirits. When a mother asked her son in spirit, "How do you live your life, Alex?" He flippantly replied through me, "One day at a time." I was surprised by this answer and thought that it sounded a bit trite. However, his mother, Diana, told me that her son had lived his life in just that way, one day at a time. He had mastered the art of being happy each day. She told me that she and her husband had even discussed that maybe what Alex had been teaching them while on earth was to live life one day at a time, just like he did.

Spirit SUMMARY

When someone we love dies by accident, being angry about it is understandable. On the surface, it seems as though a precious life has been stolen by a momentary lapse in judgment or a random series of coincidences. However, kids in spirit encourage us to look *below* the surface and see accidents as opportunities to explore the deeper meanings of life, love, and forgiveness. Kids who have died "accidentally" inspire others to effect changes on earth that not only gives their lives meaning, but may protect other kids from dying in a similar way.

4

Who's Your Daddy?

When Bloodlines Matter, and When They Don't

Spirit TWEET

"The beginnings and the ends of the bridge are in heaven. You on earth are the span between." (Said by a son in spirit to his father on the Father's Day just past.)

Spirit THOUGHTS

A Basket of Questions

"Hi, I'm Abigail and I'm adopted," the towheaded girl with the pixie haircut said whenever she was meeting someone. Abigail was my sister's best friend growing up, and her parents were friends with mine. During the adoption process, my mother and father wrote reference letters for Abigail's hopeful soon-to-be parents. They did the same for longtime church friends who adopted another little girl, a cousin of mine by marriage. As a kid, I didn't give much thought to where babies came from, adopted or otherwise. In fact, I assumed that Abigail arrived at her home much the same way that my first kitten arrived one

Easter morning—in a basket. How and why adoptions happened weren't a concern while we were young. However, when one of the adopted girls I knew became a teenager, she wanted to learn more about her birth family. Questions like, "Why didn't my mother want me?" "Do I have any other sisters or brothers?" "I wonder if I look like my mother or my father?" began to intrude on everyday conversations. The matter of fact, "I'm adopted," became the demand, "I want to know *why* I was adopted."

A need for belonging can become a sense of longing despite the loving home an adopting family provides. These fundamental questions may go unanswered for years and in some cases, a lifetime. *Does this all get sorted out in the afterlife?* Let's see what the young in spirit have to say.

My Two Dads

He was dressed in a rocker tee and had a crew cut. One of his arms was wrapped protectively around the shoulders of the woman next to him. She had long, black hair with a few streaks of white framing her face. They were an obvious couple and were sitting in the front row at an event.

I was slightly startled by the sudden presence of a young man in spirit who rode in on a motorcycle. He drove right up the middle aisle and sat idling next to the couple in the front row. That's all the information I had, so I asked if they knew a young man who liked to ride a motorcycle. The man answered, "Yes, that's Ryan," and the woman started to cry. The first thing Ryan said was, "Let's get this party started." The man confirmed that Ryan used this favorite phrase whenever any situation started to get *too* serious. It was also confirmed that riding a motorcycle was the last thing that Ryan did before he died. Ryan wasted no time and got right to the point. "I love you, Mom," he said to the woman. "Please tell Dad that I'm okay." I paused for a moment when I realized what I had just said. If the guy sitting next to Ryan's mother *wasn't* his father, then who was he? Ryan addressed my question by drawing my attention to the man in the front row and saying, "Thanks for being my dad." Then he held up two fingers. When I gave the information just as it had been given, I must have looked extremely puzzled. The man in the front row explained in a choked voice, "Ryan is my wife's son. He and I had a rough time because he really loved his father. A week before he died, Ryan told me that he was glad that I was his father number two. For an entire week, he called me 'Dad Number Two.'" From heaven, Ryan still called him "Dad Number Two."

Talking with Ryan reminded me that our definition of family has changed dramatically over the years. These days, it is increasingly rare to find an extended family of parents, children, and grandparents living in the same household. Now the extended family includes blended families of ex-spouses, stepparents, half siblings, children adopted across a cultural divide, and children conceived with love and the help of today's advanced scientific methods. Fortunately, spirits in heaven keep up with the times. Intricate family relationships may create logistical, and sometimes emotional, challenges here on earth. In heaven, however, kids enthusiastically embrace *all* permutations of "family."

Brotherly Love

For a medium, these convoluted family trees can provide more than a few confusing moments. During a phone session with a young woman named Alexia, it took nearly forty-five minutes before she acknowledged the first person who showed up for her. "I have a young girl here for you," I said when she first sat down. "She gives me the feeling of a sister connection."

"I don't have a sister," Alexia said.

"Well, I don't know what to tell you then," I replied. "There's a girl here who seems to be about seven or eight, giving me a name that sounds like 'Dan' or 'Don.'"

"Dan is my father," she acknowledged. But she still did not acknowledge the girl in spirit who claimed that she was a sister. During our time together, a number of friends and relatives visited with Alexia. As we were nearing the end of the session, Alexia's grandmother on her mother's side stood with the girl, showed me a picture of the Grand Canyon in my mind, and said "family" in my ear. "Your grandmother, Ida, is giving me the feeling that that there is a split in the family and she's showing me the Grand Canyon," I said. "The family photo that she's showing me is being ripped to pieces before my eyes."

"I understand all of that," Alexia said. "The last time I saw my father was during a family trip to the Grand Canyon. Immediately after we got home, he left my mother and me to live with another woman. My mother tore up all the photos from that trip."

Grandmother Ida, in her own way, was trying to introduce Alexia to her half sister, despite her resistance. Alexia finally acknowledged that she had heard that her father went on to have a family.

It was then that the girl in spirit said, "You always wanted a sister." At that point Alexia confessed that when she was young, she had dreamed about having a sister. She had wanted a sibling because she hated feeling lonely. "I came to meet you today because we didn't have a chance before. I want you to know that I'm with you," the girl went on to say. There was a long pause on the phone. At first I thought the line was dead.

Then Alexia's words squeaked out until her voice rose to a crescendo. "I heard that my father had a daughter with this other lady and that the girl died. My mother said that my father got what he deserved. And now you're telling me that I'm supposed to be a sister to a *half* sister I've never met?"

It sounded as though Alexia wanted to reach through the phone and grab me by the neck. We sat there for a moment quietly. I asked those in spirit to give me the right words to say. "I'm not telling you to be or do anything, Alexia," I said. "I do find it interesting, however," I went on, "that it is your mother's mother who brought the girl here. Your sister is reaching out to you with your grandmother's blessing. Of course, it is *your* choice whether to allow her into your life or not."

The phone clicked. Communication was severed. I don't know what happened to Alexia. What I do know, though, is that both sides of her family came to visit her together. Her sister came in spirit projecting the feeling of a sister, not a *half* sister. She seemed to want to emphasize the wholeness of the relationship, not the halfness created by the division within the family.

Alexia's sister was one of the first spirits to ignore the divisions that *we* create in families. She was certainly not the last.

As mentioned previously, there is a spirit protocol I adhere to as policy when I do larger events. I've developed an organizational procedure with the spirits, which helps me identify who's who in private sessions as well. When those in spirit approach me, I ask them to divide themselves with Father's side to my left and Mother's side to my right. Siblings and peers stand in front of me or next to the person receiving messages. Where a person in spirit stands in the room helps me to know their relationship to the person on earth whom they've come to see. On one occasion I saw a spirit standing across the room in a corner diagonally across from the lady sitting with me. He gave me the name "Brother John." I gave this information to the lady along with where Brother John was standing in the room. She laughed and said, "When my brother John was alive, our views on life, death, and family were diametrically opposed." As Brother John continued to communicate about the differences between their life choices, he started walking closer and closer until he was standing right next to his sister. When he reached his destination he said, "I love you anyway." It seemed to me that John was demonstrating that sharing his love in spirit literally diminished the distance between them.

In addition to where the spirits stand, they'll indicate relationship by either popping a word into my mind like "mother," "father," "husband," "son," "daughter," etc., or by giving me a feeling in my heart of what the relationship is. I've learned to identify what different relationships feel like. There have been numerous instances in which I've said something like, "A lady is standing close to me where Mother would stand. She gives me the feeling of grandmother." In cases like this the lady in spirit may turn out to be a grandmother who was like a mother to the person receiving the message. But sitters are often quick to correct me when I describe a man to a T and then call him "husband." "Oh no," they'll say. "He's my *ex*-husband."

Spirits don't refer to themselves as "ex," "half," or "step" anything. They simply identify themselves by their primary relationship to the sitter. All legal prefixes and suffixes are dropped unless a point needs to be made. During a group event a young man in spirit showed up behind a man in the audience and said one word, "junior." That was it, so I had to pass on the information. The man sat back in his chair and didn't say anything for what seemed like forever. He and the spirit were obviously men of few words. The man finally said, "My son and I share the same very long name, except for one difference. His has a 'Jr.' on the end. We called him 'Junior.'"

Exes and Ohs

One of my favorite memories is when a woman's three husbands showed up at an event at the same time! Even though two were exes, and they were all spirits, each one proceeded to comment on everything going on in her life as well as her children's lives. The group had a laugh when one of the exes said, "You told me to 'go to hell' lots of times, but I went to heaven instead." The woman said, "I came here tonight wondering if it was possible to hear from my first ex-husband, the father of my children. I was worried that we might be separated in heaven as we were on earth. It is comforting to know that *all* my husbands are still looking in on me and my daughters."

People who were not legally married during their time together on earth may give me the feeling of being a husband or wife during messages. One woman seemed perplexed at first when I referred to a man in spirit named Dennis as her husband. In my mind, he showed me a picture of a wedding dress with the international symbol for "no" superimposed over it. (Spirits will often use both common symbols and symbols specific to my understanding as a kind of shorthand.) "Well," I said. "Dennis is giving me the feeling of husband despite no wedding dress." She laughed and said that although she and Dennis hadn't legalized their union, they used to say that they were more married than most people who had a wedding license and wedding photos.

It might be assumed that since exes aren't relegated to their own section in heaven, and spirits know about one another, that family secrets might be falling from heaven like raindrops from the clouds. Well, don't be concerned. When the spirits speak with me, they provide only the information that is essential to their purpose in coming. They're not interested in passing along gratuitous gossipy tidbits (as much fun as that could be).

Apples Never Fall Far from Family Trees

In recent years, there's been a growing interest in researching family history. This interest seems to encourage spirits hidden in the family line to come forward and introduce themselves. Kids in spirit are particularly interested in meeting even the most obscure relatives because in meeting them, the age-old question, "Where did I come from?" gets answered. Practically speaking, though, sessions with lots of unknown spirits can be very irritating for a medium. This was particularly true when a son in spirit brought his newfound relatives to meet his mom.

"I don't know any of the names you're giving me, except for my son's," Carol said during a phone session. I could hear the frustration in her voice. "All I can tell you," I responded, "is that your son is holding up a tree and the names are on it." Then I felt prompted to ask her, "Is anyone in your family doing a family tree? Your son gives me the feeling that these people are on your father's side of the family. He's met them in spirit."

"That's impossible," Carol responded. "My father was adopted so we don't know his side of the family at all."

"Why not wait and see," I suggested, rather than arguing with her. It was probably about two years later when Carol contacted me again. Unbeknownst to her, a younger sister went on a mission to discover more about their father's side of the family. Some of those names mentioned years earlier did indeed show up on her family tree.

Family trees remain intact in the afterlife, despite how and why we may lop off branches on earth. Kids in spirit seem particularly interested in those lopped-off branches. In cases of adoption, there may be lots of branches of the family tree just waiting to be grafted onto the larger tree.

As a child, I spent as much time as possible in the mountains around Woodstock, New York. I would lie on my back gazing into the canopy of trees above me. I loved to watch the oak and birch trees swaying in the wind; it looked as though they were dancing. With my eyes, I would start at the trunk and follow a branch to a smaller branch and then an even smaller one. As the branches decreased in size it became more difficult to separate them from the small branches of the next tree. When I think about families in heaven, it reminds me of these forests. Spirit families create a shelter around the earth. Each person can be recognized individually as a branch while still being connected and intertwined with the entire forest.

DNA-Tested Theories

One day when I opened the door to my office, a woman stood there clutching a boy-sized stuffed teddy bear that was fully dressed in a T-shirt, jeans, and sneakers. As I invited her in to sit down, she did so, refusing to let go of the bear. Her name was Susan and she introduced me to the bear whose name was Buddy. I really didn't know what to make of this, but I have learned to not blink an eye at any memento someone might bring to a private meeting. After one session in New York, the sitter asked me if I could guess what was in her bag. Before I could answer, she unzipped her purse and a tiny, furry head popped out. After her son's suicide, she had bought a dog for comfort and companionship. That dog went with her *everywhere*, even to see a medium.

As Susan sat before me, the room began filling up with people in spirit, more than I knew we could speak with during the session. In my mind I asked for the spokesperson in the group to come forward. In response, I saw a young boy, not much bigger than the bear, standing next to Susan. Although I couldn't see him clearly, I could tell that his skin color was different from Susan's. Despite this fact, he gave me the feeling of "son."

When I told Susan that I had a boy in front of me coming in as a son but with a skin color different from hers, she nodded. Her little boy stood like a little man by her side. When I mentioned that to Susan, she confirmed that she had referred to him as her "little man" and that he was always very serious and extremely well behaved. This little boy was so mature in his demeanor that it was a bit unsettling. I'm used to kids in spirit running around and acting like kids. In his very serious way, he let me know that he was meeting lots of members of his family in heaven, those he never knew. He wanted me to tell Susan that his entire family thanked her for taking care of him. I figured that this probably explained the crowd with which he came.

After about forty minutes of details being given to me, all of which Susan understood, this little man showed me a movie in my head. In my mind's eye, I saw two flower gardens side by side, one in which a seedling looked stunted and the other that looked completely barren with nothing growing in it. The stunted seedling hopped out of the ground and jumped into the other garden plot, transforming it. In an instant the seedling grew tall and green and the garden became lush. I heard in my head, "Thank you for giving me a place to grow." When I shared this with Susan, she said that her son's favorite nursery rhyme was, "Mary, Mary quite contrary, how does your garden grow?" Although I'm sure that he was indeed referring to the rhyme, I knew that he was showing us so much more.

As Susan was preparing to leave, she told me that she had adopted a special-needs child who had numerous congenital ailments that made him small for his age and contributed to his early passing. Her special child, named Kevin, was also of a different race. Susan used Buddy the Bear as an ingenious way to explain adoption to Kevin. Susan asked her son if he loved Buddy even though he looked different. When Kevin said, "Yes," Susan said that she loved him even more than he loved Buddy. Although they all looked different from one another, they were still a family. As Susan was leaving, she said, "Even though Kevin was with me for only a little while, he changed my whole life."

When Susan and Buddy the Bear left, I sat quietly for a while, thinking about what had been said. I knew that Kevin had been attempting to provide a broader understanding of life from the spirits' perspective. Sometimes a series of smaller insights received through a number of experiences brings about a change in perception. However, because kids in spirit tend to be extremely forthright, I have many instantaneous "aha" moments when working with them. After what "little man" Kevin showed me, I understood that his soul got what it needed to grow by moving from his biological family to an adopted family. He needed the DNA of one family line, but the nurturing of another. The combination of the two created a hybrid life needed for himself, the unknown relatives he met in heaven, as well as the mother who adopted him on earth. In Kevin's situation, Susan's nurturing served his nature, helping to evolve and transform his life—and hers—for eternity. What really struck me about the garden picture was that the seedling moved *on its own* from one garden to another. It wasn't abandoned by one garden—or sought out by the other. Changing gardens is the choice of the seedling. It could be that adoption, which seems random from our perspective, isn't random at all from the spirits' perspective. Aha.

While working on this chapter today, a young marine in spirit reminded me that the idea of adoption extends well beyond family and even death. This marine managed to bring about our meeting due to a last-minute change in my schedule. Anyone who knows me can tell you that I can be a bit of a control freak when it comes to my schedule and the organization of my life. However, I've learned to be flexible with the spirits because I trust that their understanding of "what is needed and when" well exceeds my own.

Five minutes before the final meeting of the day, I opened my door to two men, one older with a magnificent mustache and one who looked to be in his early thirties with large, soulful brown eyes. My schedule stated that there was to be only one sitter for the final appointment of the day. Before I could make a mental note to discuss this with my assistant, the younger of the two males said, "Hi, I scheduled the appointment for myself, but my uncle, Jean-Louis, is in town and I thought he might need it more. I'll just wait in the car." "Not a problem," I blithely responded.

Jean-Louis didn't know what to expect from a session; he had never done anything like this before. Although Jean-Louis spoke English very well, he had a lovely French-Canadian accent.

It wasn't long before a young man in spirit appeared next to Jean-Louis, standing at ease in a military dress uniform. He gave me the name "Matt," and I passed it and the military connection along. "Matt was my son," Jean-Louis replied. "Well, he's telling me that he re-upped more than twice. Honor and loyalty and fighting for his country were more important to him than his life, " I continued.

"Yes, that's true," his father said. "Matt even wrote a letter explaining his devotion to the Marines using those exact phrases. We found the letter after he died during his third tour of duty."

Matt went on to tell me that he died doing his best to protect the men of his squad, some of whom also died during that same mission. Matt mentioned a get-together for his platoon, which his father had recently attended. During this ceremony, Matt's service was honored. Jean-Louis confirmed all of this information was correct. Matt told me that his dad wears jewelry to commemorate his commitment to service. Jean-Louis removed a medallion from his neck to show me; it was called a father's medallion. This medallion had an American flag on it. I paused for a moment considering that a French-Canadian father had a son who died while serving with the U.S. Marines.

The thought didn't linger because the messages Matt was giving me took an abrupt turn. He mentioned his extremely large family and two sets of twins, one fraternal, two identical. "My mother had thirteen children," Jean-Louis said. "Matt's right, four were twins, identical and fraternal."

"Matt is *extremely* interested in the family, those with him in heaven and those still on earth," I told Jean-Louis. "He's mentioning two young boys, sons, who are especially important to him. He's giving me the idea that he didn't know the youngest well at all and almost missed meeting him," I relayed to Jean-Louis.

"That's right," he agreed. "Matt's youngest son was one week old when he was deployed to Iraq the final time."

"Matt is telling me that he always wanted a daughter. He's talking about his *new* daughter," I said, realizing how illogical that sounded as soon as the words were blurted out. "It's very important to him that she knows he will be taking care of her every day of her life," I continued because Matt hadn't stopped talking. Jean-Louis's eyes filled with tears.

"Yes, that's right," he said. "Matt now has a daughter; the adoption is final." Jean-Louis looked across the table at me and explained, "My son wanted to adopt his wife's daughter from her first marriage. Even though all the paperwork was properly filed, it took time to work its way through the system. It wasn't until just recently that his wife received notification that his wishes were fulfilled." Matt had made it very clear that he was aware that his actions to adopt while still on the earth were completed.

Matt's final message was that he is staying close to his father, meeting relatives in heaven, watching out for his brothers-in-arms, loving his boys, and protecting the daughter who now carries his name.

After Jean-Louis left, I thought about our time with his son. It seemed to me that Matt was more concerned with the legacy he left behind on earth than about his own life. He had committed himself to a nation that wasn't his by birth, was adopted into the brotherhood of the Marine Corps, valued his place within his father's family line, has two boys to carry on his bloodline and a daughter who is his legacy of love. *Wow*, I thought. This guy jumped from garden to garden while leaving footprints behind in each one. Matt was very much at peace, his many legacies secured.

Matt shared his legacies with me in a very direct and determined way, much the way he pursued his goals while on earth. Sometimes, however, the spirits resort to theatrics to get their points across regarding family legacies. One evening at a home circle, men in spirit stood in line behind a young man sitting in the living room. The line of spirits was so long that it stretched through the living room and into the kitchen. The last few spirits seemed to disappear into the refrigerator. What was so dramatic about all these men was that they all had fiddles and were playing away. When I mentioned this to the young man in the room, he informed me that he had come from a long line of well-known Irish fiddlers. Not long after all the fiddlers in his family came to visit, the young man went on to record a collection of traditional Irish tunes that had been written and played by men on his father's side of the family.

In the case of the Irish fiddler, the legacy of music was well defined and passed along from father to son. In situations where a son dies before his father, the natural order of primogeniture seems to be irrevocably interrupted. However, a young man in spirit surprised his father (and me) with what he had to say about his family's legacy.

Bridging the Gaps

Rick is tall and looks intimidating, especially as he studies you through his black-rimmed glasses. He's extremely fit and has an I-just-finished-running-a-marathon type of confidence. When Rick and I sat down together on the day after Thanksgiving several years ago, he leaned forward in his chair, cast his eyes downward, and barely said a word for the next fifty minutes. A teenager in spirit named Jeff identified himself as Rick's son. Jeff had lots to say, thankfully, because his father wasn't saying a word. Jeff brought another spirit with him, a female family friend who said that she had passed by suicide, a choking suicide, and thanked Rick for helping her husband deal with her choice. The spirits were chatting on and on and yet there was barely a grunt from Rick.

When the session was over, Rick asked, "Do you want to know who I am and why I'm here?"

"No," I said, "no more information is necessary."

Rick ignored my answer and proceeded to explain that he had worked with afterlife researchers who had suggested that he meet with me. Rick excitedly recounted point by point how accurate the information was that the spirits had provided.

After that visit, Rick contacted me about every six months to visit with his son, his father, and people he knows in spirit who stop in to say "hello." What I enjoy about repeated visits is that I have the opportunity to experience how the visitors both in this life and the afterlife grow and change. Afterlife relationships are as dynamic and changing as relationships in this life.

As the spirits and sitters become more comfortable with one another and a history of communication is established, we can begin to explore more complex concepts of life, death, and the afterlife together. These interactions are what really keep me interested in the process of spirit communication because it begins to touch the greater purposes of this communication and life itself.

During a recent phone session on Father's Day with Rick, both his father and his son in spirit came to visit. Rick's father is an extremely unemotional, military-minded tough guy with an intense interest in World War II. Rick and his father did not have an affectionate relationship here on earth. Rick's father viewed any emotion other than anger as a sign of weakness. In sessions past, Rick's father had apologized for not being a loving and supportive father. Rick's relationship with his own son, Jeff, was very different from the one he shared with his father. Rick and Jeff were the best of friends. They joked together and had a great time. Jeff appreciated life's (and death's) ironies. When Jeff died so young, Rick lost not only his son, but also his best friend and his legacy. Jeff was an only child and with his death, that limb of the family tree would grow no more branches.

At the beginning of this Father's Day session, Rick's father said that he considered the past all water under the bridge. This just seemed like a trite phrase until both he and Jeff started talking about bridges again, but this time in reference to a new military man in Rick's life who was an engineer, a bridge builder. Rick acknowledged that by volunteering with a hospice organization, he had come in contact with a hard-bitten army man who reminded him very much of his father. This man had been in the Corps of Engineers, the bridge builders of the army. Rick's father informed him that he was also helping the engineer by inspiring Rick with thoughts about how to break through this man's hardened crust. Rick said that he and the man's own son were amazed at the ways in which this tough guy was finally opening up, sharing his feelings with those closest to him for the first time ever. Rick's father thanked Rick for working with this army guy (even though he had been a navy man in his time, and the two groups are notorious, though respectful, rivals). Rick's father told him that the healing brought about by this relationship on earth was allowing the limitations of their own relationship to become "water under the bridge."

It was then that Jeff, Rick's son, jumped into the conversation and dropped entire phrases into my mind. "The beginnings and the ends of the bridge are in heaven," he said. "On earth, you're the span between. What you do there has its beginning and end here with us. What you do on earth reaches us in heaven, and we're changed."

That statement stopped us all for a moment. I had always considered myself and other mediums as bridges between those living on earth and those living in heaven. The way I saw it, one end of the bridge was on the earth and the other reaches into the afterlife. Jeff was using the bridge analogy in a new, and much more profound, way.

After speaking with Jeff and Rick's dad, I'm compelled to reconsider the way I've been looking at bloodlines and legacy. The father's legacy is the son's . . . and the son's legacy is the father's as well. Our lives here span from the past to the future, from earth to heaven, through time to endless eternity. What we do here on earth has its beginning and end in heaven. Another "aha."

Did You Say Forefathers or Four Fathers?

Not *all* members of the younger generation I encounter are living in the afterlife. More and more young people on earth are coming to see me because they want to learn about the life beyond this one. At first I was confused by their interest, because kids, on the whole, don't think much about death. But what I have come to understand is that kids on earth actually consider the spirits as part of life, so asking for help to hook up with the spirit world or to deepen a connection they already have with the spirits is perfectly natural to them. I receive an increasing number of e-mails these days from parents who don't know what to do with a child who is seeing and talking with spirits as a matter of course. The pressure to teach mediumship development to teenagers has really increased.

After years of talking with such communicative kids in spirit, it no longer surprises me that kids here wish to communicate with others in spirit too. Kids are simply inclined to keep in touch. When kids text and tweet each other on earth, it's a lot like the constant communication I experience with young spirits who also have a desire and need to express themselves and be heard. Kids, both here and there, take for granted that we're all interconnected in some way. The many new modes of communication available to kids on earth today actually mirror the way kids in spirit are able to communicate naturally—with speed, ease, and reach. It's just a matter of time before we are all talking to each other across worlds so accessibly. A word in today's vernacular sums it up for me. Sweet.

With such increasing interest in spirit communication, I wasn't phased when a member of this very communicative generation set up a meeting with me. I made no assumptions about why, but was stunned when the first thing that popped out of my mouth was "You have four fathers." I was sure that I had just made an embarrassing faux pas. "Yes, I do," the twenty-three-year-old named Walter replied. My sense of relief was brief because the four male figures in spirit were crowding in on me, talking at the same time. It was a confusing melee until they separated themselves by distinguishing characteristics. One was extremely tall, one was smoking a joint, one was bald, and another spoke German.

The German man, Gunther, was the first to communicate. He was Walter's birth father, and he had died in a skiing accident before Walter was born. He and Walter's mother had had a fling when she spent the summer in Switzerland on a work-study program. They hadn't gotten married.

The extremely tall man was Walter's grandfather. When Walter's mother returned home unwed and pregnant, her father became a stand-in for Walter's birth father. Walter called him "Big Daddy."

The joint-smoking dude was his mother's first husband, Walter's stepfather. This dude had gotten arrested for dealing pot and died in prison.

The bald man was an old family friend who was Walter's godfather. He had carefully overseen and financed Walter's education. He passed suddenly with a heart attack just two weeks before Walter came to see me.

Each of these men considered himself Walter's father. Each expressed a continuing interest in his life. Each of these men made it clear that they are aware of each other in spirit and the part they play in Walter's life. Two are related to Walter by blood, one by marriage, and the other by commitment. As Walter was leaving that day, he thanked me. "Today heaven gave me back my fathers," he said with a smile. "All four of them."

Heaven gives back our fathers, our mothers, our children, our sisters and brothers, those we know, and those we don't. In heaven, family is defined by more than bloodlines. Family is defined by love lines, too.

Spirit ANSWERS

Are there orphans on the other side?

Absolutely not. *Everyone* has family in the afterlife even though family ties on earth may be completely severed. Orphans on earth are also not alone. Death doesn't deter parents from seeing to their children's welfare. This year alone, thousands of children have lost both parents because of war or natural disaster and are completely bereft because of it. But after terrible disasters, I often hear stories about how people—some with families of their own—are moved to adopt a child (or several from one family so as to keep the children together). I can't help but think that parents in spirit are inspiring loving families to take care of their children in ways that they no longer can.

No matter what happens to separate families on earth, there are reunions in heaven that help bind them all again. Innumerable spirits have told me how delighted they were to have been embraced by family members they hadn't met while living on earth. No one is an orphan in heaven. And no matter how it may appear at times, no one is orphaned on earth, either. No one is ever really alone in this life . . . or in the afterlife.

If I don't know who my father is, how will he find me in heaven?

First of all, just because you don't know who your father is doesn't mean that he doesn't know who you are. Secondly, just as there are distinctive physical family characteristics on earth, such as a Roman nose or a particular manner of walking, there are also energetic similarities between family members. Although the physical body no longer exists in the afterlife, these similarities of energy allow for immediate recognition.

When you die there is no need to worry about how you will find family members and those you love. It is *their* job to find you.

Spirit SUMMARY

Today's families are often an extended conglomerate of former spouses, stepparents, half siblings, and in-laws. With adoptions on the rise, the modern concept of family extends well beyond cultural, religious, and genetic lines. Kids in spirit bring harmony to what may otherwise appear to be a confusing mess of broken relationships. They define families as souls connected not only by DNA, but by choices, some of which have been made by the kids themselves. Although legal relationships may dissolve on earth, in heaven love remains—and grows.

5

By My Own Hand

Kids in the Afterlife Talk about Suicide

$\mathscr{Spirit}$ TWEET

"Would there be any reason good enough?" (Quote from a nineteen-year-old in spirit when his mother asked him why he took his own life.)

$\mathscr{Spirit}$ THOUGHTS

Suicidal Thoughts

While dreaming during a November night years ago, I heard what sounded like the pop of a firecracker. I awoke with an acrid taste in my mouth as though I had been chewing metal. The taste remained throughout the day, no matter how I tried to camouflage it with other strong flavors.

I was used to having strange dreams and assumed that this one, like the others, was a nighttime expression of my daytime interactions with spirits. The disjointed images or convoluted storylines usually faded by the time I brushed my teeth in the morning. Rarely did a taste invade my reality for an *entire* day.

This dream was different in a way that I didn't understand. On Thanksgiving Eve several days later, I finally understood.

The night before Thanksgiving, my handsome blond-haired, blue-eyed, slightly younger cousin Tommy stood outside his ex-girlfriend's house, proclaimed his undying love for her, and then shot himself. He was nineteen.

My aunt asked me to sing at the funeral, but singing seemed like an impossible response to the situation. The music of my own soul was suddenly still, as still as I imagined his body to be. My ears, usually attuned to the gentle harmonies of heaven, were deafened by the sound of a single gunshot, the gunshot that had killed him.

Suicide. This word slams into the chest with the frustrating finality of someone having the last word in a cosmic argument. With suicide, any opportunity for discussion or negotiation dies as well, or so I thought at the time.

Maybe by boycotting the funeral I was boycotting my cousin's choice to die. Yet even this action of distance (or defiance) on my part couldn't slow the questions spinning in my head like horses around a manic carousel.

"Why did he do it?" I asked myself. "Why didn't he call me?" "Why didn't I understand the dream? Shouldn't I have seen the signs?" "What more could I, should I, have done?"

During this time of my life, I was still recovering from a severe car accident while taking a break from a grueling academic schedule. The accident not only left me in pain and with physical problems, which still persist today, it also brought a sudden influx of intense and uncontrolled sensitivities. There were times when my life seemed too much. There were moments that I, too, had considered the option of dying. Although I chose to stay here on earth, my cousin didn't. And I wanted to know why. Why, why, why?

My search for answers drove me to religious texts, scientific studies, and pop psychology magazines. These days it is much easier to find information about suicide on the Internet. The U.S. Centers for Disease Control and Prevention website states that suicide is the third leading cause of death for youths ages fifteen to twenty-four. These are staggering statistics made all the more staggering when someone you love is one of the percentage points. What the CDC can't possibly measure is the effect that suicide has on the people left behind.

Suicide seems like the ultimate rejection—of everyone and everything. It feels very personal and personally directed because someone we love has made a choice to be somewhere else rather than be with us. At least, that's the way I felt when Tommy took his own life.

I . . . was . . . angry.

When Tommy died, I was still inexperienced in dealing with spirits and understanding how things worked in the afterlife. My lack of knowledge caused me to be terribly afraid for his welfare and unsure of whether we would or ever could be together again. What I didn't know then was that rather than explaining himself *directly* to me, Tommy would heal our relationship by introducing me to kids who, like him, chose when and how to die.

I talked to a friend yesterday who asked how the book was coming along. I responded by telling her about my cousin, Tommy. "Surprisingly," I confided, "tears blurred my vision and dripped onto the keyboard while writing about his suicide." Even after all these years, just thinking about him brought back intense emotions from that heartbreaking time. Apparently, emotions don't have an expiration date.

The reaction I've had to writing about Tommy has helped me understand why kids in spirit seem to be particularly resistant to using the word "suicide" . . . especially when their parents are sitting in front of me. It only brings back the painful memories, not the good ones. Of course, whenever I think I've got things all figured out, kids in spirit remind me that I'm always learning and that there are exceptions to every rule. Therefore, I shouldn't have been surprised when a young man in spirit whispered "suicide" in my ear just before I started relaying messages at a small group gathering this afternoon. He pointed to the lady sitting next to me.

The pointee sitting to my right was very well put together. By that I mean that her hair was perfectly curled, the color of her clothes matched, her purse and shoes were coordinated, and her jewelry completed the ensemble. She was the *last* person I wanted to say "suicide," to, but the young man kept prompting me to do so. "I have a young man standing behind you with a J name who says, 'suicide.'" With that statement, all of her controlled perfection dissolved before my very eyes and her crystal blue eyes filled with tears. "That's my son, Jeremy," she replied nearly choking on the words. "There was talk that his death was accidental," I continued, "but he's telling me that *you* were right. It was suicide."

There was silence in the group; no one breathed. And no one moved either, until someone passed the box of tissues to the perfectly coiffed woman.

"I knew my son had killed himself," she whispered, "even though people kept saying that his death was an accident." By spurring me on to use what I thought to be a harsh word—"suicide"—her son, Jeremy, was actually reinforcing what his mother knew to be the truth. Well-meaning people may have tried to shield her, but instead of helping, this deception created loneliness in her knowledge. Jeremy, on the other hand, was speaking from a place where truth is always a greater expression of love than any lie could be.

"Jeremy loves to party," I told his mother. "He had a struggle with drugs, though, one that he couldn't overcome."

"Yes," she acknowledged.

Then Jeremy talked about seeing his mother reading his words, his poems. He told her that his reasons for dying were in his writings. He never felt at home here in this world, he told me. He always fought for the underdog and didn't like the way that people treated each other. Eventually living on earth was just too painful for him. When I passed all of this along to his mother, she replied. "I understand. He wrote about these feelings in his poems."

Then Jeremy shifted the course of the communication very suddenly. That's the way it is when talking with kids in spirit; you have to learn to keep up! "Jeremy loves to surprise people with gifts," I said.

"Oh yes, he was always doing that."

"Well, he's brought a surprise here today, a man with an *A-l-l* name, which sounds like 'Allen.'"

"*Allen?*" shrieked Jeremy's mother. "That's my husband, Jeremy's father!"

I went on, "Jeremy says that he and his father had a difficult relationship on earth, but they're together now in heaven."

She turned to me wide-eyed and said, "That's why I'm here

today." When she paused to take a breath, she also wiped the tears from her eyes. "I needed to know that our family could be together again someday. When Jeremy committed suicide, I thought that he was lost . . . forever."

Oh no. Absolutely not. Suicide, although an expression of alienation, doesn't create eternal separation. Instead, kids in spirit who have passed by suicide use the experience to open up a dialogue with us about life, responsibility, love, and relationships—the very things we may think that suicide destroys. As far as the kids are concerned, suicide isn't a conversation ender. It is very often where the conversation of healing begins.

Learning to Talk Again

During the early years of my work, I was invited to visit a picturesque tourist town in California to conduct some small groups and private sessions. I was very excited because this was the first time I was on a road trip to talk with spirits. As I drove into what looked like the perfect setting for a Western film, I thought, *Why do they need me here? This place looks as though it is the ideal town.* The red barn at the outskirts of the city, with its horse-shaped sign reading FEED and all the T-squared storefronts lining Main Street, sealed the impression. But during my first group session I was soon to discover that even "perfect" towns have suicides.

"Tell my mom that I'm alive, I'm sorry that I hurt her, and I love her!" exclaimed a spirit named Nick who had killed himself at age twenty-two. The details he gave to me about his life included his desire from the time he was a little boy to be a police detective just like his dad. He talked about his red bicycle, his favorite cowboy hat and cap gun, the family trips to the fair, and his prom date. And then he apologized to his mother, Doris, for his sudden, seemingly unpremeditated death by his own hand. But instead of providing an explanation for his choice, he intentionally reminded his mother of the good times that they had shared together. He thanked her for baking a favorite strawberry cake on his birthday year after year and mentioned that his birthday was just a couple of days away. He wrapped up his visit by saying, "Dad and I are a lot alike. We handle things the same way."

"*That's* true," Doris said through clenched teeth. It wasn't long before I learned just how similar they were.

Doris's husband, Gus, was the next person in spirit to speak. Every bit the retired detective, he was a determined man, organized in his thinking and very precise in the way he communicated with me. His barrel chest and solid stance contributed to his formidable presence in the room. He made it clear from the start that he was a man of action. "Once I made up my mind about something, I just did it," he told me.

"That's his way," Doris agreed, her teeth just slightly less clenched.

Gus then walked me through his final moments on earth. I was seeing things from his point of view—waiting until Doris had left for town. Walking to an outbuilding on the property. Arranging things to create the least mess possible, so that Doris wouldn't be left to clean it up. Barricading the door so that Doris wouldn't find him. The gun. The last thoughts of Doris. Like his son, this self-possessed retired metro detective killed himself.

"I love you, Doris. I still walk along the stream with you every evening," her husband then said. There were no words that could adequately describe the love that Gus was giving me to pass along to Doris.

Doris, the wife and mother who had been left behind so dramatically and definitively by both husband and son, sat stoically and emotionless on the sofa, acknowledging all the details of the messages I relayed to be true. All the details, except one. I don't think that she believed her son and husband loved her, because, in her mind, if they had, they would have stayed.

The next morning I felt led to attend a small yet vibrant church right off Main Street. I was looking forward to experiencing the comfort, peace, and tranquillity that small town churches so often provide.

Right after the service, when I was feeling all warm and fuzzy, my arm was gripped hard and I was spun around to face Doris, the detective's widow. "I have a bone to pick with you," she said in a low growl. "I'm *so* mad! How can my husband and son say that they love me? They left me here alone! How dare they! How dare *you!*"

Needless to say, I was startled. As I took a breath, I asked for help from the spirits. "It is natural to feel angry," I responded. "I know what it is like to lose someone very close in just this way." I reminded her then that her husband's final thoughts were of concern for her and that he continues to walk with her each evening. I reminded her that her son spoke about the good times. And then frantically, I searched for the minister of the church.

Doris's emotions were extremely raw. It seemed as though feelings she hadn't been able to express for years were now being released with the violence of a sudden summer thunderstorm. I wanted to enlist the support of her minister because I knew that she would not only need help now, but certainly in the days ahead.

In Doris's situation, the suicides of her son and husband had been conversation enders. I learned later that prior to receiving messages from her son and husband, she refused to speak about either of them or their deaths. It is clear that for Doris, suicide was a conclusion—the end of their lives *and* hers, the end of memories, the end of joy, and the end of all talk. But those in spirit who loved her wanted to restore life, memories of good times, and even hope. They wanted to begin the conversation of healing.

Some months later, I heard from Doris's minister that the encounter with her son and husband did indeed start Doris talking. She talked and talked and talked. She eventually got beyond her anger and reclaimed her life. Starting the conversation was the beginning of her long-term healing.

It was also the beginning of my relationships with pastors, psychologists, psychiatrists, and therapists. Oddly enough, I had visited this small town at the request of a psychologist who was receptive to spirit communication. In the years to follow, a number of mental health-care professionals have sent clients to me. A few of the braver ones have even presented workshops with me. I, in turn, recognize that although mediumship is a valuable part of the equation that ultimately helps bring about healing, it cannot provide the ongoing support required in dealing with all grief. As was the case for Doris, loved ones in spirit frequently start a conversation through me that continues long after I leave town.

Who's Responsible Now?

It's often challenging to reclaim our own lives after we lose someone we love. Suicide seems to make it all the more difficult. But those who end their lives on earth soon discover that they haven't stopped living at all. And none of them expect *us* to stop living because of their choice. So what makes it possible for us to go on? Here's a true story that might provide some clues:

When a father in spirit came to visit his daughter, her outburst in the middle of the session startled me. "When he killed himself, he killed me too!" she shouted.

"Don't own my death!" he shouted back from spirit. "It's mine, not yours!"

At first the words seemed petulant, two people staking a claim on one death. This unrestrained, somewhat impolite exchange was surprisingly cathartic for the young woman, however. She and her father had argued prior to his suicide and she was sure that her actions had prompted his choice. By shouting back (and continuing their argumentative relationship) her father wanted to make it clear that his daughter wasn't responsible for his choice.

"I get it," she said after our session was finished. "His death really isn't about me."

Like this father, kids in spirit don't want those left behind to own their deaths. One of the great ironies of working with kids who have died by suicide is that we here on earth often learn about responsibility from *them*. Personal responsibility seems to be one of their mantras—for them and for us. Although kids may mention contributing factors like drug or alcohol use, relationship problems, and hopelessness, I haven't heard one kid in spirit blame a parent, sibling, friend, or anyone else for their final action on earth. What seems like an irresponsible and self-ish choice often provides a spirit with an opportunity to take full responsibility for the whole of their life's choices, even if one or more of their choices resulted in their death.

Kids in spirit talk a lot about having wanted to be free while they were here on earth. Suicide is often an expression of that desire to be free—free from the constraints of life, free from the pain of conflicted relationships, free from the responsibilities of being responsible.

Once they're in heaven, though, they speak of discovering a very different kind of freedom than what they expected. Instead of finding freedom by disconnecting from others, they find freedom by connecting to themselves—by owning their experiences, actions, and choices, by assuming responsibility for them, and by recognizing that we are meant to live in relationship and interdependence with others on this side and the other side. "In heaven there's no place to hide," one young man told his mother. "I see myself clearly."

One young man in spirit named Ryan showed me that after he hung himself, he woke up in a house of mirrors, surrounded by reflections of himself. While on earth, he had hated the way he looked, so much so that he had no mirrors in his room and avoided them whenever possible. He even went so far as to mutilate himself with razors and sharp objects. He had died trying to escape from himself and instead found he was now face-to-face with all aspects of himself—seeing himself quite literally from all angles. Heaven, for him, was like a funhouse, he told me. There were tall Ryans, short Ryans, fat Ryans, and skinny Ryans. "Just images," he said. "Images that are always changing." What wonderful perspective he now has!

When kids die from suicide, they not only get to see themselves with new eyes, but they become aware of the full impact their passing has on everyone who knew them. From the casual acquaintance who then decides to embrace life more fully to the parents who are devastated in mourning, kids in spirit hear it all and see it all. Nothing shields them from experiencing the full impact their lives and deaths have had upon others. One teenager who shot himself in the woods came to me with an apology for the kids who found him. He was aware of the effect that discovery had on them.

The most stunning admissions from those who have taken their own lives come from the spirits who once believed that their family and the world would be better off without them. Thankfully, they report that this limited and limiting viewpoint dissolves with death.

Feeling the Love

I was surprised a while back to hear a teenager who had killed himself talk about all the ways he had created mayhem within his family. Usually kids in spirit want to talk about happy times. But this young man went on to say that he had caused his mother great distress when he started stealing money for drugs. He confessed that he believed he was responsible for his parents splitting up and for his little brother's beating at the hands of a drug dealer.

After he died, this young man was finally able to see and accept the love that had been extended to him by his family all along. "Mom, your love was a gift that I didn't know how to open," he said. (In my mind he showed me a beautifully wrapped present tied up with rainbow-colored ribbons and bows.) He continued, "I brought your gift to heaven and opened it here." I described the image he showed me of a heart bursting out from within a wrapped box.

"Does he really know how much I always loved him?" she asked me with pleading eyes.

"Absolutely," I assured her. "Your son showed us here today that the saying 'you can't take it with you' doesn't apply to love."

The love and compassion that we offer to those who have died by their own hand affects their experience in the afterlife. Love elevates the spirits. A fifteen-year-old girl who had died after taking an overdose of prescription medication told me that her mother's love lit the path toward heaven for her. Her mother later told me that she wondered if her daughter could see the candles that she had been lighting for her in church daily. This mother was sure that her love would illuminate the way until her daughter was able to see the light of God's love directly. I'm sure, too.

For the Record

One of my favorite cities is Laguna Beach, perhaps because it feels less like a city and more like a big beach party about to happen. The sun seems to always shine with purpose there and radiate throughout the rest of the world as an afterthought. It is always somewhat bewildering, therefore, to meet grieved parents when I visit this bright place.

On a particularly sunny day, I opened my hotel room to a man and woman I had imagined to be the quintessential Laguna couple. He was outfitted in shorts and a T-shirt, and his face was framed by reddish curls. She was tall, leggy, and supremely tanned. Her long blond hair fell well below her shoulders. We made our introductions and headed for the seating area in my room. In just a few words, I detected English accents. I had a little laugh at myself for making assumptions, something I teach my students *not* to do! In many ways, I find sessions by phone preferable to meeting in person, because I'm less apt to be distracted by the way people look.

As the couple, Steve and Jane, sat down and got comfortable, I inserted a tape into the tape recorder and rested it securely on the broad arm of the sofa. Just as I finished my opening blessing, the tape recorder *flew* off the arm of the sofa. Steve jumped and exclaimed, "No one touched it!" From his perspective that might have been true. But from mine, I could feel the energy of a young spirit trying to announce his presence.

I set the recorder back in its spot, only to have the same thing happen again. This time, it broke. "Well," I told the couple, "it doesn't look as though we're going to get a recording of our time together."

For some reason, the spirits find recorders irresistibly fun to mess with. For example, one mother, excited to play her session for her nonbelieving husband, called me to ask if I would check my recorder again. "Nothing on the tape can be understood," she said. "Sometimes you sound like Minnie Mouse and at one point you're talking backwards! My husband said that this is impossible."

"Didn't your son mention that he was going to do the impossible in order to show his dad that he's around?" I reminded her. By the way, I checked my recorder and it was just fine. Moreover, none of my other clients had complaints about their tapes.

As Steve, Jane, and I studied the broken recorder, I could feel their son standing in our midst. In my mind, he showed me a garage filled with vintage cars and gave me the feeling of joy around those cars. When I mentioned this to Steve, he responded with, "I have a vintage car collection and business. My son used to love to help me keep the cars shined and ready to go." The young man kept saying, "Bray, Bray, Bray" in my inner ear, and his parents confirmed that indeed his name was Braydon. He had a lovely sensitivity and thoughtfulness, which I mentioned to his parents. Braydon impressed me with his creativity and love of music. He wanted to be a musician and showed me a picture in my mind of his mother reading notebooks of his lyrics. Jane acknowledged that she sat in his room at night, reading those lyrics for clues. "Clues to what? To your death?" I asked Braydon in my mind. "How did you die?" I didn't get a response, so I accepted that our conversation was going to be a one-way affair.

Once Braydon was sure that his parents knew beyond a shadow of a doubt that he was with us, he went on to say, "I'm not blaming anyone for my death. I'm taking responsibility." I had the sense that he had ended his own life. Although he didn't give me any details, he showed me a snapshot in my mind of a bed with a striped bedspread. When I passed along this information, Jane's eyes seemed suddenly lit by a fire about to be extinguished by tears. She started wringing her hands while telling me that her son had committed suicide in the bedroom with the striped bedspread. She was the one who had found him. Jane was relieved to hear that he took responsibility for his own death. Because of an argument they'd had on the day of his passing, Jane had been blaming herself. Despite her relief, she still wanted to know more. In a hoarse whisper she asked, "Why?"

I pushed against the back of my chair and took a breath. I explained to Jane that I would ask the question, but I doubted that Braydon would answer me (especially since he didn't seem interested in answering anything I had asked him up to that point.) In my mind I asked, "Why, Braydon, why?"

Braydon responded so suddenly that it was as though he had tossed a brick through the window of my mind. And then I realized that the brick he threw wasn't an answer, but a question.

He asked, "Would there be any reason good enough?"

Now it was Jane's turn to sit back and take a breath.

"You're right, Braydon," Jane said. "*No* answer would be good enough."

Braydon's question remained with me throughout the day and into the evening. That night as I got into bed, I thought about my cousin Tommy. Decades had gone by since the Thanksgiving Eve of his death, and still I asked, "Why?" Braydon's question, however, quieted mine. Braydon had reminded me that explaining death, no matter how it comes, doesn't bring healing from grief. Frankly, there will never be a reason good enough for a mother or father to lose a child, at least one that they are willing to accept. Rather than reasons, Braydon brought the offer of relationship, one that continues despite the choice of suicide and beyond our desperate quest for answers. It wasn't until months later, that I realized my cousin, Tommy, had been trying to do the same thing . . . for *years*.

Surprise Visit

Ahh . . . the Bahamas. The promise of warm ocean breezes, beaches of white sand, gentle waves of aqua water, and reggae in the streets. Everything *is* better in the Bahamas . . . even spiritual retreats. Every spring for seven years, I taught spirit communication and provided messages for groups gathered from around the world at a resort in this glorious environment.

One of the great joys of these weeklong events is meeting and working with other mediums. It is truly an international group, but one with a singular mission: to help people understand the principles of spirit communication and demonstrate the healing that the work can provide.

One year, a striking husband and wife team from Switzerland joined the teaching team. Eva was as lovely in her demeanor as she was in appearance. Her long, thick, pure white hair was swept into a single loose braid down the center of her back. She moved gracefully, her lithe figure seeming to waltz with every step. In contrast, Matthias, Eva's husband, was leonine in appearance. His wild, curly, salt-and-pepper hair framed his face and a thick beard obscured nearly all of his face except for his eyes. Because of his imposing appearance, the twinkle in his eye can easily be missed. That is, until something strikes him as funny and he *ho ho ho*s with more enthusiasm than Santa Claus.

As I taught my morning classes, Eva and Matthias took notes—*copious* notes. It looked as if they were writing down *everything* I said. Frankly, it made me nervous. Their reputations as leaders in mediumship preceded them, so I wondered, "What on earth could they be learning from *me*?" I mentioned my trepidation to Matthias and he threw back his head and laughed. "We are always learning," he said, quoting Michelangelo. I've worked with many wonderful mediums through the years and they all share a surprising trait . . . great humility. That was certainly on display here.

All week I looked forward to seeing this lovely couple work together, but my interest increased significantly after I learned that while Eva provided messages, Matthias drew portraits of the spirit with whom she was communicating. I simply couldn't wait to see that!

The big night finally arrived. I sat toward the rear of the room with the other retreat facilitators. We all attended each other's events during the course of the week so that our collective energy would enable the best connections possible for the retreat participants.

Toward the end of the evening, Eva stood quietly for a moment with her eyes closed. Then she began to speak in a gentle, almost girlish voice. "I have a young man in spirit here just under twenty years old," she said. "He died of a broken heart. Oh no, wait, please . . . he had a broken heart, but he died by a gun. He shot himself." There was whispering throughout the audience and then silence as Matthias started to draw. A roundish face emerged beneath a mop of blond hair in the illustration taking shape on the art pad.

"He is showing me a uniform, he was in the American forces," Eva said while Matthias continued drawing furiously, his body blocking the easel and sketchpad from full view.

"Does anyone know this young man?" Eva asked. No one said a word.

"Let's see what else he can tell us," Eva continued. "Oh, he loved music and played the guitar. The person he is here for also loves music and was a musician, maybe a professional one." My heart started beating rapidly and my palms became sweaty. My cousin Tommy had been in the navy. He loved music and was learning to play the guitar before he died. Music was one of my majors in college and I had been a professional musician for a number of years. *Wait a minute*, I thought. *This can't be Tommy. I'm here to help people on this retreat, not to get a message myself.* I continued to dissuade myself from the possibility that Tommy could be talking with Eva. And then it happened.

Matthias stepped back from the easel and there was a sketch of my Tommy, a beautiful blond-haired, blue-eyed young man.

"I know this young man," I said. And then I started to cry to the point where I couldn't stop.

Of course I didn't have any tissues with me. I wasn't expecting to hear from my own loved ones. Fortunately, those who had been expecting messages had brought packs of tissues, which they hastily shared.

But Tommy wasn't finished with me yet. "This boy is your cousin, but like a brother, yes?" asked Eva. "Yes," I replied. "He wants you to know that he helps you with your work. He brings the spirits to you, those who died like he did. He knows that you can help them and their families."

"Thank you, Eva," I managed to say between choking tears. And then I blew my nose.

It might seem strange that I hadn't been communicating with Tommy directly throughout the years. The work of spirit communication is funny that way. There seems to be a fail-safe built right into the system preventing mediums from being in constant contact with their own loved ones. Mediumship is a work of service, not self-service. The truth is that mediums need mediums, too.

That night when Tommy visited Eva, he evidenced a relationship that I thought had ended with his suicide. Through each young person he brought to me over the years, he taught me about love, compassion, forgiveness, personal responsibility, and clarity of vision. While I thought the healing was for their families and friends, it was, in part, for me too. He had been my silent partner for all this time. That night, with my newfound awareness of his presence, our conversation began . . . again. As did our work together.

Spirit ANSWERS

Does God get mad at you for taking your own life? Does he see that as his job?

Although the spirits haven't talked to me about God's being angry with them per se, they readily acknowledge the anger of their families, friends, and coworkers. A guy in his twenties, who had committed suicide immediately after launching an Internet business with a friend of his, said this to her during a session: "I know you're pi**ed that I didn't keep my promises." I was surprised by this statement because usually my interactions with the spirits are G-rated.

"He has no idea how pi**ed I am," she responded.

"Oh, I think he knows," I told her.

A beautiful girl who had died from anorexia at the age of twenty-one told her parents, "I feel God's love here. I couldn't accept that God loved me when I was on the earth. I accept it now." This was a great relief to her parents, who were churchgoers and were concerned that her death, which could be viewed as a slow form of suicide, would have put her on the wrong side of God.

Adult spirits will often talk about the choices they made throughout their lives, which contributed to their deaths. One man who died from complications of alcoholism told his son,

"I killed myself one drink at a time." A father who continued smoking cigarettes despite suffering with emphysema told his daughter, "Some people choose to die all at once. Some of us just take our time." One mother in spirit apologized to her daughter for not keeping her diabetes under control; she died quite young from a heart attack as the result of her choices. "Oh, she refused to stay on her diet and didn't monitor her sugar," the daughter told me. "She wouldn't listen to anyone who tried to help."

I met a young soldier in spirit who died while saving members of his platoon. In a split second he made the choice to die so that others could live. His family was grieved by his death, but also proud. His fellow soldiers and their families were grateful. This young soldier summed up his choice by saying to me, "I did what I had to do. I didn't take time to think about it."

When I spoke with a man who had hung himself in his barn, I was surprised to hear him say, "I thought my family would be better off without me." His son was outraged by this statement. "How could Dad think that way?" he asked. In an odd way, this father had believed that his death was an act of self-sacrifice.

We're given tremendous latitude on earth regarding how we bring about the end of our time here. However, it is our responsibility to become more aware of how our choices impact others. It is our job to make choices in a conscious way, rather than an unconscious one. Life doesn't just happen to us; we make life happen. It is often the same way with death.

If you kill yourself, do you have to sit outside of heaven until the time you would have naturally died?

Many people, including some mediums, believe this to be true. Fortunately, in my experience with spirits, none have reported being stuck outside the gates of heaven. This caused me to wonder why my experiences differed from those of some other mediums. When I asked for help in understanding why this might be, I received an answer from a young man in spirit who clarified things a bit. He told me how he tried helping another man in spirit, who had killed himself, accept the fact that he wasn't exiled from heaven because of his actions. But the spirit who had killed himself wasn't buying it. After this encounter, I had to consider the possibility that if someone believes his actions alienate him from God and all the blessings of heaven, that belief in itself can create his reality in the afterlife. Another thing I've learned from listening to spirits is that they are aware of our thoughts and what we say about their deaths, good or bad. It follows then that if loved ones on earth keep saying that his actions will keep him from entering heaven, he will sit outside the gates and wait.

I think that it is important to note that as a medium I don't have all the answers. In fact, my work is a bit like putting a puzzle together. At first there are lots of puzzle pieces scattered all over the table. As more messages are received, puzzle pieces begin to fall into place. Over the years as I've spoken to the spirits about many topics, including those in this book, the puzzle pieces have started to resemble a more complete picture. One of the reasons that I love working as a medium is that I'm curious. I am eager to see the whole picture—if not today or tomorrow, then someday.

Do spirits who have committed suicide feel remorse?

People who have died from suicide often express deep sorrow for how their choices have affected the people closest to them.

However, these spirits aren't the only ones who come with apologies. There are some days when it seems as though the only message from the spirits is "I'm sorry for (just fill in the blank)." When one woman's husband died, she discovered that he had borrowed against the equity in their home and lost the money in a failed business venture. When she came to see me, she was facing imminent foreclosure. Needless to say, her husband said "I'm sorry" a lot.

How do other spirits treat those who have killed themselves?

The answer to this is simple: with love. More often than not, spirits who have died by suicide come to visit loved ones here on earth with other family members in tow. They are not ostracized by the other spirits. Of this, I am sure.

Is there judgment for taking your own life?

In the afterlife, each of us must take full and complete responsibility for *all* choices made while living on earth. Some spirits have told me that it wasn't until after they died that they fully understood how their actions affected themselves, others, and—not to sound dramatic—all of creation. One young man who killed himself said, "I was living in my own little world. When I ended it, I didn't know that the bigger world would not let me ignore the one I had created." He was a very philosophical kid who had ultimately realized that he couldn't escape what he had created with his life, that he finally had to face it.

Living in a physical body is of tremendous value and provides an opportunity for accelerated spiritual growth. The importance of our life on earth is underscored by every spirit who comes to see me. Lost opportunities cause the greatest regret of all in the afterlife. I'm not talking here about items on a bucket list like "Climb Mount Everest" or "Sail down the Nile." The spirits demonstrate tremendous interest in how we live our lives and what choices bring love, hope, and healing. And the spirits *always* weigh in on the side of life.

I've spoken with kids in spirit who have actually encouraged a parent to remain on earth. I shouldn't have been surprised to discover that many parents had thoughts of suicide following the deaths of their children. But despite the obvious pain they knew their parents were going through, not one kid in spirit has supported an option of suicide. One teenage boy went so far as to say, "Stay on earth, Mom. You keep me alive there. Plus you've got lots of work to do."

One woman even said after a session, "I wanted to hear from my dad that it was okay for me to die now. All he talked about was my life and how he was helping me through it." Yes, that's right. The spirits encourage us to stay here on earth; they *are* helping us through it.

In thinking about the spirits' perspective on life, Google Earth came to mind. The spirits are zoomed out and can see the world, the countries, the states, the cities, the streets, and the people all at once. They can see all the possible roads to take, the places to visit, and the people yet to meet. We, however, are completely zoomed in as we can only physically walk down one road out of the many available to us. It is easy to think that there is only one road while we are walking on it, especially if it is a road of physical or emotional pain. These are roads that seem to have signs that say "dead end." One of the reasons why the spirits come to visit is to remind us that *no* road is a dead end. From their perspective there are many roads, and all of them say "help available."

Knowing that the spirits are with you is a bit like having a triple-A card on the road of life. When you get stranded, help is only a call away. There is a reason why people feel inspired to call a suicide line during a time of crisis rather than pulling a trigger. The spirits always encourage and inspire us to stay on earth.

Dying isn't a problem solver. In fact, with help from the spirits, living can be and often is a problem resolver.

Spirit SUMMARY

Suicide not only leaves behind broken hearts, but unanswered questions as well: "Why did you do this? Why didn't you ask me for help? Could I have done something to make you stay?" But all these questions only succeed in adding to the grief experienced when someone we love takes his or her own life. For this reason, it is not surprising that kids who have made this final choice also make an extra effort to let us know that they have survived. Although heaven isn't denied to someone who commits suicide, spirits experience the ramifications of their actions on earth and are fully aware of how their choices have affected others. Where there are unanswered questions about death, kids in spirit bring unexpected answers about life. When suicide creates a deafening silence, kids in spirit start the conversation again. They are determined to bring us clarity on this issue, for their own sake as well as the sake of others.

6

We Shall Overcome
Addictions in Life and Death

Spirit TWEET

"Sometimes healin' comes with dyin' . . ." (Spoken by a
young man in spirit who died from a heroin overdose.)

Spirit THOUGHTS

Sobering Thoughts

"Do I *have* to talk to him?" Ingrid asked midway through our
session, her lips pressed so tightly together that another word
couldn't have been pushed through.

"Of course not," I replied while being tugged on by the spirit
in question.

A spirit tug feels like a real tug. Sometimes when there's a
strong pulling sensation on my arm I'm surprised that no one
else in the room can see my sleeve move. Spirits of *all* ages do
the tugging, even though it feels like a toddler trying to be noticed by a distracted mother. Other times there might be a tug
on my proverbial heartstrings or my right ear feels like one end

of a taffy pull. In the case of the spirit wanting to talk with Ingrid, I was being tugged on in all three ways. "Okay, okay," I said in my head. "I get it. This message is important."

Ingrid was seated next to the door of my hotel room, as far from me as possible. She had purposely positioned herself sideways in the chair with her feet pointed toward the door. I half expected her to bolt from the room at any moment. When she first entered, I had noticed that her tanned face was deeply lined, but that her bright, cornflower-blue eyes were lit with the energy of a woman half her age.

Ingrid's daughter, Marthe, was seated in a chair between her mother and me. She looked to be in her mid to late forties, and although still youthful, she seemed more world-weary and worn than her mother. In the seat nearest to me was a very pretty young woman with long, dark curly hair. She was pregnant—so pregnant, in fact, that I was concerned any emotional upset might precipitate labor. I didn't know whose idea it was to meet with a medium, but as things progressed it was obvious that it wasn't Ingrid's.

While I would have preferred to ignore the spirit standing next to her, as *she* clearly never wanted to talk to him again, I couldn't. The continuing tug on my heart wouldn't allow it. Besides, his insistence reminded me that my agreement is with those in spirit. It is my role to give them a voice, even if someone doesn't want to listen.

With that in mind, I took a deep breath and decided to ease my way into things by talking with one of the other spirits standing next to Ingrid. As it turned out, she was Ingrid's older sister Emily and luckily she began things off on a lovely note; Emily thanked Ingrid for taking care of her as she was dying with cancer and Ingrid, in turn, thanked Emily for taking care of her when they were little girls. But soon thereafter Emily turned to the impatient man in spirit standing with her. That's when the visit started to go awry. The man looked red and roughened, as though he had been standing in a biting wind for hours. He gave me the name "Jack." That's when Ingrid asked me if she really had to talk to him.

At times like these, I feel more like a mediator than a medium.

"Of course not," I replied. "But would you consider listening to what he has to say since your sister, Emily, brought him here?"

"Okay, I'll give him a minute," Ingrid said, somewhat begrudgingly.

I wasn't ready for what came next.

As soon as Ingrid agreed to the communication, I was washed away by a tsunami of alcohol. It was as though the entire room was adrift in a sea of cheap whiskey. At the same time, Jack flashed the image of a picturesque barn into my mind's eye. My heart became heavy in my chest as though it would burst with sorrow. "I was a mean drunk," Jack said. "I'm so sorry. I'm so sorry for *everything* I did."

I didn't know what "everything" meant. But I knew that whatever had happened in that barn brought tremendous misery and pain to anyone who had passed through its doors. There seemed no doubt that alcohol abuse was a major contributing factor.

I hesitated for a moment before sharing all of this information. I was concerned that the emotional tenor of the message might have a deleterious effect on the women, especially the young, pretty mother-to-be.

However, my work agreement with the spirits doesn't come with censoring privileges. I've agreed to provide the information I'm given, nothing less, nothing more. If a sitter asks me "Have you told me everything?" I'm never in the position of having to reveal something that has been held back.

Without finessing the information in any way, I presented it to Ingrid. An expletive exploded in the room.

"He has a *lot* to be sorry for," she spit out.

"I get that feeling from him," I said. "That's why he's here . . . to apologize."

"Apology not accepted," she retorted. "My father started drinking in the morning and by the time Emily and I were home from school, he'd be on a tear. He took to beating us in the barn, daily. Emily used to make me go and hide and she'd take the beating for me. It was an awful way to live. One day when he didn't come after us and didn't come for dinner, my mother made me go to the barn. There was my father, dead right there on the ground with the whiskey bottle still in his hand. 'Good riddance' was my only thought."

Ingrid's torrent of words seemed to have no effect on her father, except to make him more determined. He was still tugging on me and not willing to give up. "Forgive," Jack whispered into my ear.

"Do I *have* to forgive him?" Ingrid asked me. "Because I don't want to," she said emphatically, crossing her arms over her chest and inching closer to the door.

At that moment I noticed a different man in spirit leaning against the wall between Ingrid and her daughter. He gave me the feeling of both husband and father. I smelled cigarette smoke, saw a red-and-white pack in my mind's eye, and was given my symbol for beer drinking, which is a mug being lifted and tilted. I turned to Ingrid's daughter, Marthe, and said, "You have a father in spirit who drank and smoked when he lived on earth. He's showing me a red-and-white pack, so I think he smoked Marlboros."

"Yes, my father smoked Marlboros and drank beer," Marthe said.

"He sure did," added Ingrid.

Oh no, I thought. *Here we go again.* That thought was punctuated with pain in my side and back, which is what the spirits give me when communicating liver and kidney failure.

Marthe said, "My father died from a combination of liver and kidney failure. He basically drank himself to death."

Before I could consider the similarities between the two male spirits in the room, a third caught my attention. He was standing between Marthe and the pretty young woman.

"There's a young man in spirit here as well," I said. "He looks to be about nineteen or twenty. He's writing a *J* and an *R* in front of my eyes, so those may be his initials."

"That's my husband, JR," the pretty young woman gasped.

"That's my son," said Marthe. "The *JR* stands for 'junior.' He has the same name as his daddy."

"That's why we're here," said Ingrid. "To talk to JR."

JR's first words were, "I don't drink."

"That's right," his mother said. "JR saw what drinking did to his daddy; he refused to ever start," she continued proudly.

For one so young, JR seemed very mature in his thinking. Although he had a forceful personality, he was extremely gentle as he spoke to each of the women in his life. He thanked his grandmother for helping him buy a car. He thanked his mother for taking care of his wife. He joked with his wife about their baby boy's name by saying, "His name better not be Junior, Junior." His wife actually laughed as she remembered that he said that very thing when they first learned that she was pregnant.

Then JR got serious. In my mind, he showed me a picture of an old-time saloon. On the bar, a cowboy hat sat alongside a thick textbook. Marthe confirmed that JR always wore a cowboy hat and worked in a saloon at night to help pay for college classes. JR showed me closing the bar for the night and getting in his car. Then a series of impressions overcame me, as though I were riding on a roller-coaster ride. I saw trees flying by me, a curve in front of me and then I felt an abrupt shift in direction as though I were being pushed from the side. JR had been blindsided, literally, by another car speeding onto the highway. He wanted his family to know that his passing was sudden, swift, and painless. What startled and puzzled me, though, was that I smelled alcohol in the midst of the accident.

After I passed all this information along to the three women who loved him, the only one able to speak was his grandmother. "JR was killed by a [expletive] drunk driver," she said, barely able to keep her anger under control.

JR, a beautiful young man with a family who loved him and a baby on the way, had made the choice not to drink. He was determined to create a different life for himself and his family. Yet despite all of these good choices, his life on earth was still ended by alcohol abuse.

I was stunned for a moment when I realized that I was sitting in the room with five generations, each of which had been affected by death related to alcohol.

JR broke my brief reverie with three words, "forgive, hope,

help." In my mind's eye he showed me a picture of himself holding a baby.

When I mentioned this, Marthe said that she had always told JR that he was their only hope that alcohol would lose its grip on the men in the family. Now that JR was dead, she said, there was no more hope.

"Oh, I don't think that's true," I said to Marthe, "otherwise JR wouldn't give me the word 'hope' while holding a baby, his baby.

"Forgiveness, hope, and help," I iterated.

Just as we were about to end the session, the three male spirits closed ranks by Ingrid's side. I felt the tugging again, this time as though my heart were being pulled from my chest. I heard *forgive* in my inner ear again with the force of love behind it. "Ingrid," I said, "your father is standing next to you with your husband and your grandson. I'm feeling tremendous love and hearing the word, 'forgive.'"

"No," she said, and walked out.

Meeting Ingrid and her family left a profound impression on me. Although I have met many other families ravaged by generations of alcoholism and other addictions, none has affected me quite as much. What made this encounter so memorable was not only that five generations were engaging with one another *in the same room*, but that this was the first time I saw spirit communication as *more* than a way to help heal grief. The spirits were determined to use communication as a cooperative tool for transforming life for past, present, and future generations. In Ingrid's session, what started out as a warm reunion with her sister ultimately became an opportunity to transform the entire family's relationship to alcohol and to one another.

Alcoholism had stolen hope, happiness, and, in some cases, life itself from each generation in the family. Although death had not diminished JR's determination to change the future, his willpower alone couldn't break his family free from the connection to alcohol abuse. It seemed to me that the triumvirate of fathers in spirit were standing in unity to demonstrate that this transformation was to be a group effort. However, Ingrid wasn't ready at that moment in time to hear that message or to change the story of her life. She wasn't ready to accept that the key to transforming the destiny of future generations often requires forgiveness and the inclusion of past generations' help.

Ingrid seemed convinced that forgiving her father would help him in some way and she wasn't about to do that! But the urgency of the tugs on me, coupled with the love I was feeling from the spirits present, convinced me that Ingrid's choices from that day forward could not only affect her own life, but that of her unborn grandchild as well. Of course, Ingrid's free will gives her the option of accepting or rejecting what the spirits had to say.

As a medium, my role in people's lives is limited. I learned early on that although I can share messages from the spirits, I can't be attached to the effect that information might have. When Ingrid walked out of the room, I had to let her go whether I perceived that there had been healing or not. My one consolation, however, is that after years of working with the spirits, I know that just being in the presence of their love effects change, even if it isn't noticeable at the time.

Spirits can perceive even subtle changes in our thoughts. From their point of view, the smallest shift in earthbound thinking can eventually bring about complete transformation.

I think this is why spirits are patiently persistent in their communications. It is because they recognize that infinitesimal changes in the present can dramatically affect the entire family's story for all generations.

The spirits want to help write a different ending to our story, because our story is theirs as well. Years after meeting Ingrid, another young man in spirit showed me how a story much like hers can have a very different ending.

Breaking the Cycle

Pat had given my kitties lots of attention when she arrived. (I have an instant rapport with people who love animals.) We had chatted about different rescue organizations, holistic medical options, and pets we had loved and lost. Pat was outgoing and relaxed and seemed very comfortable in her own skin. Her demeanor was that of a person who hadn't a care in the world.

But Pat's sister, Mary, was entirely different. Mary was so tense that her shoulders were at the same level as her earlobes. She seemed irritated by our casual conversation. Up to that point, her contribution to the conversation consisted of "hello."

As soon as we sat down together, I smelled alcohol and cigarettes. It wasn't emanating from the ladies sitting across from me, so I knew that it was coming from the spirits. I also experienced a dizzy feeling that I often get when there is a spirit near me who had suffered from drug addiction.

"Wow," I said to Pat. "I smell alcohol and cigarettes, and there is also someone in the room who passed under the influence of drugs."

"That makes sense completely," Pat said, in a voice that was almost too cheery. Mary's eyes grew wide behind her glasses.

"The first person visiting here today is a father or a father figure," I said. I heard the nursery rhyme "Georgie Porgie Puddin' and Pie" in my ear. When I mentioned this, Pat laughed and said that her father's name was George. It was a family joke to sing this nursery rhyme to him because he loved old-fashioned porridge, chocolate pudding, and apple pie. Well, I knew by the smells in the room that those weren't the *only* things that George liked. "I smell unfiltered cigarettes and your father is showing me a camel. He smoked Camels, didn't he?"

"Till the day he died," Pat answered.

"He's also bringing with him the smell of alcohol, and I hear the name 'Johnny.'"

"'Johnny Walker is my best buddy,' my father used to say," Pat explained.

Pat's father George showed me his navy uniform and the Buick that he loved so much. I heard a "pop" sound in my head, which usually means that someone passed with an aneurysm. I mentioned this to Pat and she said, "We don't really know how my father died, but the doctor thought it was most likely an aneurysm. He was found sitting up in his chair with a cigarette burned down in the ashtray and a bottle of Johnny Walker by his side."

You might think that because I recognize unfiltered cigarette smoke that I've been a smoker myself. Actually, I've never smoked a cigarette. However, after years of working with spirits, I can even recognize the packaging of different brands. I know the difference between cigar, pipe, filtered, and unfiltered cigarette smoke. Spirits who were heavy smokers will arrive in a cloud of it. I've experienced the pain of lung cancer; I've felt my lungs fill up with fluid as though I'm dying from congestive heart failure.

When the spirits first started giving me such vivid memories,

I sometimes had to ask them to "take it away." In the course of my work as a medium, I've experienced so many ailments that it would have been easy to become a hypochondriac. In one instance, I was coughing so hard I couldn't catch my breath and had to shift in my chair to breathe better. "You're sitting just like my father did in his last days," the sitter said. Her father had died from emphysema.

After years of experience, I am now rarely overtaken by the feeling of addictions and death conditions. The spirits give me just enough of a smell, a taste, or a pain for me to understand what they're trying to show me.

These experiences have become so much the norm that I sometimes forget to tell people that their loved ones in spirit are no longer suffering with either the addiction or the death condition. I explain it this way: Just imagine that you're driving through a neighborhood where you used to live. When you see your old house, you decide to stop in and have a visit. As soon as you walk through the door, you might be flooded with memories of years spent in that house. That's the way it is with the spirits. When they're visiting with us here on earth, the experience is like visiting an old house. Often when they draw close to me, the first memory that they'll share is the last memory that they had on earth—the memory of the way they died. In that second I'm reminded that spirits are no longer suffering, they are just remembering.

I explained to Pat and Mary that although their father brought the familiar smells of smoke and alcohol with him, that didn't mean that he was still smoking and drinking in the afterlife. Pat said that she understood and seemed surprisingly okay with all of this. Mary remained silent.

George interrupted my explanation by giving me a picture of a house in my mind's eye, with a "For Sale" sign in front. There were two little girls standing with suitcases in the driveway. He gave me the state name Ohio. Mary gasped. "Because of my father's drinking," she said, "he lost his job and we had to sell the house. My sister and I were sent to Ohio to live with our grandparents."

"Thank you for forgiving me," George said to Pat.

"I didn't forgive him until after he died," Pat said. "I'm glad that he knows."

Spirits often refer to events that have taken place after their deaths. By mentioning these things to a medium, it reminds their families that they are still involved with their lives and check in to see what's happening.

George directed my attention to the spirit of a young man standing next to Pat. I could hear harsh music around him. He was playing a guitar that sounded like one of my cats having a very bad day. His hair was jet black and spiky.

When I mentioned all of this to Pat, she said in a matter-of-fact way, "Oh yes, that's my son. He was learning to play the guitar when he died."

"It sounds as though he is playing with a band, a loud one," I said.

"Oh, he liked *really* loud music," she agreed.

"Well, then you must like it, too," I told her. "He's showing me that you listen to his music at night before you go to bed."

"Yes, I do," she said. "I lie on his bed and crank it up loud so that he can hear it in heaven."

"He's giving me two 'A's,' as though an important name starts with them or they're initials. I'm also hearing the name 'Ron.'"

"Aaron is my son's name," Pat said with a chuckle. "He always used to make a point of telling people that his name started with a double 'A.'"

"Hi, Aaron with a double 'A,'" I said to the young man with spiky hair.

After that, Aaron and I fell into a comfortable rhythm of communication. Some spirits are good communicators, and Aaron was one. He showed me dice and the Las Vegas sign. His mother confirmed that he had always dreamed of going to Las Vegas. "He's telling me that he was in Las Vegas with you," I told her.

"Oh no," she said. "We never went to Las Vegas together."

"He is making it clear to me that he was in Las Vegas with *you*, and it feels as though it was a recent trip."

"I went to Las Vegas two weeks ago for a high school reunion. Could that be it?" she asked me.

Aaron flashed a picture of a flamingo into my mind. "If you stayed at the Flamingo, then yes, he was there."

"We *were* at the Flamingo!" she exclaimed.

At that moment, I was hit with a dizzying sick feeling, which is what I get when someone has died while under the influence of morphine or heroin. Aaron was learning how to communicate with me, but he went a bit overboard with the drugged feeling.

"Aaron was addicted to heroin. He went into rehab and tried to stop," I said.

"Yes, that's right," Pat said.

"He was clean for a while, he's telling me," I continued. "That's why it was such a disappointment when he died from an overdose."

Silent tears spilled from Pat's eyes.

"He's telling me that he died because he didn't have the same tolerance for the drug," I said.

"Yes," Pat whispered. "He used too much and died."

Aaron didn't let Pat sit there in tears. "Mom," he said. "Thank you. Thank you for loving me, for encouraging me." Then Aaron did something I didn't expect. He showed me the symbol that spirits often use to signify drinking. While doing that, he pointed to his mother!

"You were a drinker," I said to Pat. "Aaron gives me the understanding that you quit after he died. He said that he helped you, just like he's helping Ricky."

Mary let out a sound like a kitten mewing. She looked to Pat to answer me.

"Mary's son, my nephew, Ricky, is in rehab right now," Pam said. "He has a drug problem. We came here today wanting to know if there is hope for him."

It was then that I saw Pat's father move next to her son. "Your father is standing with your son. They're giving me the sense that they're both helping Ricky," I told Mary. "Your father is showing me a ladder with three rungs on it. As he stands on each rung, he paints a word on the side of a house. Next to the bottom rung he painted, 'forgive,' the one above it says 'hope,' and the top rung says 'help.'"

"Oh, that's interesting," Pat said. "My father was a house painter early in his life. He always used to say that when facing a problem, take it one rung at a time." Pat paused for a moment. After taking several deep breaths, she continued. "After my son died, I didn't want to live anymore and started drinking more and more. When my sister asked me to not leave her by dying, I knew that things had to change. I started by forgiving my father because that was the only way for me to get sober. Something changed when I took that step; I finally had hope that maybe there was a different way to live. I know that I was helped because I couldn't have done it alone."

I felt a sudden urgency from George. He wanted to show me something.

"Your father is showing me another 'for sale' sign on another house. He agrees with you that the money from the sale of the house can help with Ricky's rehab expenses—to help him live a new life."

"On our way here today, my sister and I talked about that exact thing," Pat said. "The money from the sale of our grandparents' house is just sitting in an account for us to share. I told Mary that our family would want to help Ricky and I do, too."

Mary took a breath, possibly the first one since the session began. The room became suddenly still, which often happens when the spirits are about done. "Before we end our time together, do either of you have any questions?"

"Yes," Pat said. "Is my son really okay now? Has he finally beat this thing?"

When I looked to Aaron for an answer, I heard him say, "Mom, sometimes healin' comes with dyin'."

Aaron really gave me something to think about. As much as it may be a relief to know that addictions themselves don't follow loved ones into the afterlife, the ramifications of a life lived fettered to addiction do. With dying, the insulating qualities of drugs and alcohol pass away. Coming face-to-face with the impact of addiction is a sobering thing. From their perspective, the spirits can see clearly that addictions will live on in their families unless something changes. This is why I believe that family members, even those reviled by their sons and daughters' actions, are *driven* to communicate.

After Pat and Mary left, I was reminded of my meeting with Ingrid's family so many years ago. The same words, "forgive, hope, help" were given to them. Why do people who have created havoc in our lives on earth ask for forgiveness after death? What does forgiveness have to do with hope? Can the spirits really help heal addictions?

It is easy to assume, as Ingrid did, that by forgiving her father she would be helping him only. However, after hearing "forgive, hope, help" from more spirits than I can count, I've come to realize that this triangle is nothing short of an opportunity to transform the lives of past, present, and future generations. What Ingrid and I didn't understand all those years ago, is that her father and grandson were giving *all* of us the secret formula for freedom, not just from addictions, but from all self-imposed limitation.

In previous chapters, we've heard spirits describe what heaven is like. It is a world where physical limitations are replaced by realms of *possibility*. It is also where the full impact of choices made on earth can be seen from all angles. Frankly, death is life-changing.

Here on earth we live in the world of *probability*. Insurance companies are masters at working within the framework of this world. Given certain facts of family history and current lifestyle habits, statistics can predict how long you're going to live and how much you should pay for the privilege of dying. On a daily basis, each of us looks at situations and judges what the likely outcome will be for ourselves and others. Isn't it always easier to see where someone else is going wrong? Think of it this way: The spirits have an even broader vision than ours. They want to share life from their perspective so that we, in turn, can see these visions for ourselves.

In talking about this, I'm reminded of a favorite childhood film, *The Wizard of Oz*. The film begins in black-and-white. When the twister lifts Dorothy's house, her life is spinning out of control and she can no longer determine her destination. In a sense, addictions create twisters in our lives.

However, when Dorothy's house lands, she opens the door to a world of color, a different world altogether from the one she's known. In our world, forgiveness opens the door between a black-and-white, out-of-control life into a world of color, dif-ference . . . and transformation.

Forgiveness is the missing component for *everlasting* change. To forgive or not to forgive isn't the question. It is the answer to the question "Can my life be different?" Forgiveness allows us to become aware of realms of possibility. This awareness in turn creates hope that there can be a different way to live. What is most likely to happen is replaced with the possibility that *anything* can happen. The spirits live that way on their side of death. That is the world that they want to share with us on our side of death.

It is in possibility that hope lives. The hope that the spirits talk about is not a noun, but a verb. It is an action word in an active tense. Hope is movement. It is in the activity of hope that the spirits can help.

During sessions, spirits often say that they will help with a certain person or a certain situation. This declaration is just as frequently met with a mix of relief, appreciation . . . and skepticism. A single mother came to see me, distraught about her son Caleb's uncontrollable anger. Her husband in spirit, who had abandoned her and Caleb long before his death, told her, "I will help you with Caleb." His wife responded, "That would be nice, but it is too little, too late, don't you think?" Absolutely not. Not if we open the door to possibility with forgiveness.

Forgiveness opens the door to two-way communication—without the need for a medium. During sessions, I'm often asked such questions as, "Will you tell my son that I love him?" I always respond by saying that you don't need a medium to tell the spirits anything. They can hear you! Our prayers reach them, our anger reaches them, our love reaches them.

When a very religious lady in spirit came to visit her granddaughter during a session, she said, "I pray for you every day just like I did when I was on earth." That statement really got me thinking. I had always considered prayer to be a one-way communication—from earth to heaven. What if prayer was a reciprocating process and the spirits prayed for us? What if they were sending their thoughts to us, their love to us, their knowledge to us?

I like to think of the help that the spirits provide as being prayers from heaven rather than answers to prayers from earth.

Once we forgive, once we're aware of the realms of possibility, once we start acting on hope, then we can be open to help from those in spirit.

Prayers of hope may arrive as an encouraging word from a stranger or as a schedule change, which allows a chance meeting to change your life. Forgiveness is what allows prayers from heaven to be received and your own prayers for help to be answered.

Choosing to heal while we're here on earth has implications, not only for us, but for everyone around us, those living in the afterlife as well as those yet to be born. As Aaron said, sometimes healing comes with dying . . . but it doesn't have to. Not for us and not for those who come after us.

Spirit ANSWERS

Are there guilty pleasures in the afterlife? Can you smoke or drink? Are they even considered vices there?

As the physical body passes, spirits are freed from the physical aspect of addiction. Therefore, after someone dies, he or she doesn't have to suffer through withdrawal symptoms. However, all addictions have spiritual and emotional components as well. Although no longer tied to their bodies, spirits face the emotional and spiritual attachments to their behavior without continuing to experience the chaos created by it. The shining light of heaven doesn't allow spirits to hide in the shadows of rationalization. Spirits can see the effects of addictions on their own lives and the lives of their families and friends. To repeat the words of one spirit, "Death is sobering."

Although spirits will come in clouds of smoke and waves of alcohol, this doesn't mean that they are still smoking and drinking. I like to think of these things as "identifiers," just another way a spirit defines its prior bodily self. Smoke and alcohol smells are memories, and like death conditions, are often impressed upon me so that the spirits can address the ways that their actions in life affected those left behind.

If people are drinking and using drugs, are they wasting their lives here on earth?

The spirits have told me time and again that there is no such thing as a wasted life. However, that is not to say that those in spirit don't admit to missing opportunities to live differently. Often, seeing the wreckage left behind in the wake of an addicted life calls those in spirit to help others suffering from addiction. Spirits really do want to help clean up the mess.

Do spirits have sex?

This is my favorite question of all time because most people are afraid to ask it! I hate to let you down by saying, no, spirits don't have sex, but they don't need to. Nor do they have the physical equipment to perform sexual acts. However, the spirits have something *better* than sex . . . union in love. In the afterlife, there are no physical bodies to separate one person from another. Although the spirits' energy can retain a body-like form, the essence of who they are can easily blend with someone else's energy. Spirits in heaven are connected in ways that we on earth cannot imagine. In heaven, complete union in the love of another is possible.

Do spirits take their debts with them to heaven?

In answering this question, I'm hard-pressed to come up with a single example in which a kid in spirit talked to me about leaving behind a lot of debt. In some situations, kids mention that money was borrowed to finance an education and the debt was still outstanding when they died. Even then, kids in spirit make it clear that their education isn't for naught; knowledge is something that they take with them when they die. However, what kids are concerned about when communicating with their families or peers is getting across the point that they have survived death and will continue to remain connected to those they love. The only debt they seek to repay from heaven is returning their parents' love . . . with interest.

Spirit SUMMARY

As we so often see, addictive behavior destroys relationships and lives. When a young person dies as the result of an addiction, it may seem that others in the family are fated to continue suffering. However, kids in spirit are motivated by love to replace the despair they see on earth with the hope that there is a better way to live. From heaven, kids are determined to help break the cycle of addiction in their families once and *forever*. Through the power of forgiveness, they show us that change is possible. Right here, right now.

7

Peer Pressure

How Kids in Spirit Help Kids on Earth

$\mathcal{Spirit}$ TWEET

"We're connected." (Said by a group of young men to the gang member who was responsible for some of their murders.)

$\mathcal{Spirit}$ THOUGHTS

It's Pet-ogogical
(Or: The Things We Learn from Animals!)

"I'm seeing a donkey, the rear end of a donkey and a burger. An ass and a burger. I know that sounds weird, but that's what your sister is showing me," I told Marion, a beautiful middle-aged woman sitting across from me.

As a medium, sometimes I receive information that seems perfectly ridiculous or nonsensical. Rather than interpret what a spirit is trying to convey, I've learned to present information "as is," no matter how preposterous it might seem. "Give it as you get it," is my oft-repeated mantra.

Marion had a musical laugh. The "ass" and "burger" brought forth that laugh in several octaves. "My sister always had a great sense of humor," she said. "Could she be trying to tell you that my son has Asperger's Syndrome?"

I had to award Marion's sister an A for innovation. We had indeed been talking about Marion's son and the concerns she had about his college choices and medication issues.

My visit with Marion and her sister was extremely positive and obviously, humorous. I wasn't surprised, therefore, when she signed up for a small group event and brought her son. What did surprise us all, however, was the spirit who showed up to speak with him.

"Mar-owwwww," Chi, my Bengal cat howled at the front door. I was in the process of setting up chairs in the living room for the small group event. "Mar-OWWWWW!" Chi howled again with lots of emphasis. "Welcome," I said to the spirit who entered through the door. Whenever Chi exhibited this specific howl, I knew that a spirit who died by suicide was visiting.

Chi was sensitive to the spirits ever since his kittenhood. And his vocal greeting is a throwback to the DNA contributed by the wild Asian Leopard Cat. It is chilling, distinct, and *loud*.

One reason that I'm mentioning Chi in this chapter is that he is an intrinsic part of this particular encounter with the spirits. Another is that some of you may have noticed that your own animals seem aware of things you can't see. The third reason I'm telling you about Chi is that, frankly, I was smitten with him from the first moment I saw him.

About an hour prior to the event, Chi began howling. He started again in earnest when Marion arrived with her son, Jordan, the one with Asberger's Syndrome. Jordan sat to my immediate right. He seemed shy and withdrawn and unwilling to look me in the eye. I was a bit concerned about whether the intensity of spirit energy might be overwhelming for him. I said a quick prayer asking that my helpers in spirit would also help this young man feel comfortable in their midst.

As soon as we officially started the event, Chi's howling intensified and I saw a young man in spirit standing behind Jordan. He told me that he had taken his own life. He was wearing a sports jersey and was very outgoing and charming. He gave me a name that started with a "C" and sounded like Carl.

I told Jordan what I was seeing and asked him if he knew this person. Without looking at me, he said, "No." The spirit wasn't willing to take "no" for an answer and put both of his hands on Jordan's shoulders. Then Chi jumped onto Jordan's lap. If Jordan was startled, he didn't show it. I was startled, though. This wasn't Chi's usual behavior.

"Jordan," I said. "This young man who killed himself is *definitely* here for you."

Chi settled down on Jordan's lap. Chi wasn't in the habit of settling down on *anyone's* lap, even mine.

Carl started to speak. He talked about his relationship to the family through Jordan's sister. He related how he had teased and bullied Jordan at school. He talked about a few specific instances, which Jordan acknowledged and remembered.

"I'm really sorry for treating you so bad," Carl said.

Jordan responded with, "That's okay," but Carl wasn't finished. Jordan sat in his chair, facing the floor, with Chi lying in his lap like a loaf of bread.

"Don't let anybody tell you that you can't do something," Carl continued. "You can go to school. You're a real smart guy. You can do more than anyone thinks you can."

With that statement, Jordan raised his head. He didn't look at me, or at anyone else, but he nodded. With that nod, Carl was gone and Chi jumped to the ground. We were all a bit . . . *awed* is the word that comes to mind.

Marion's sister made an appearance as well that day, but it was Carl's message that made the greatest impact. After the event ended, people couldn't stop talking about Carl, Jordan, and Chi. What a trio they made—the bully who came from beyond death to encourage the boy facing a challenge and the cat who, after announcing the presence of one of these boys, took an active role in comforting the other.

Because Chi was such an important element in this encounter with spirits, I'd like to take this opportunity to digress a bit and talk about animals, pets in particular.

In my own life, I can't remember a time when pets were not a vital part of my family. Growing up, I had birds (my earliest memories were of parakeets named Petie 1 and Petie 2), fish, reptiles (including an iguana named Ignatius), hamsters, guinea pigs, cats (Peppi, Cassandra, Nefertiti, and Cleopatra), and dogs (all beagles, for some unknown reason).

My most current menagerie is entirely comprised of felines who insist on decorating my clothing with the fur that they shed. Another less expected benefit to their presence in my life is that they help me with my work. For example, as soon as someone arrives for an appointment, Isis, a geriatric, gray Manx, limps over to make sure she's seen. Her imploring eyes say, "Pet me, pet me," and the reverberating purr in response to a head scratch brings comfort to the recently bereaved. Vandal, who cannot help but knock over anything his paw comes near (he acts like a toddler craving attention), can coax a smile even from those in the deepest grief. Rhaevan, who possesses a beautiful face and a perfectly groomed angora coat, brings order and peace to the chaos that sudden loss brings. But it was Chi, my handsome Bengal cat, who made the greatest impression on visitors.

Chi became my trusted compatriot, especially in situations when someone had died by suicide. It was therefore devastating when I was faced with making the decision to end his suffering from lymphoma. Because I did indeed make the difficult choice to release his spirit from his body, it is now easy for me to understand, and therefore sympathize with, anyone who has lost a beloved family pet.

One of the reasons why I'm inserting some thoughts about pets in this chapter is because sometimes a pet serves as a pseudo-sibling to kids in a family. They can be a peer of sorts, especially to only children. A pet can be someone to play with, someone to talk to, someone who keeps you company without telling you what to do or how to behave. Kids on earth—and in spirit—love their pets and talk about them quite a lot.

"Brandy is here," Larry, a spirit boy in his mid teens told me during a phone session. I described a black-and-white dog that I saw standing with Larry.

"I had a border collie named Brandy when I was growing up," Larry's father said, hesitantly.

"Well, Larry is showing me a picture of another border collie, one that is still alive," I replied.

"We have Larry's dog, Jam, who is a border collie," his mother said.

"Your son is giving me the feeling that he'll be taking care of Brandy while you take care of Jam," I told Larry's parents. It struck me as an odd cosmic irony that Larry was with his father's childhood dog in spirit, while his father took care of his childhood dog on earth.

"I'm so relieved that Brandy is with Larry," said his father. "I couldn't imagine my boy being without a dog." "Taking care" of a family pet is often a child's introduction to responsibility for another being's welfare. It shouldn't surprise us, then, that kids would express that continued caring while in spirit.

I've had many similar encounters with kids and pets, more numerous that I can count. I was touched by a son's concern for his parents when the subject of his dog came up. "Your son, Ethan, has a German shepherd by his side," I reported. "The odd thing is that instead of barking, I hear what sounds like an owl!" I said, puzzled. There was silence on the other end of the phone. I thought for a moment that Ethan's parents were as puzzled as I was. Then I heard a chuckle. "Ethan's dog was named Hoot," his father said. Ethan went on to tell me that Hoot had recently joined him in the afterlife. His parents confirmed that to be true. "It's okay, Mom, I'm still with you, and so is Hoot," Ethan said. In a tear-filled voice, Ethan's mother told me that she had to put Hoot to sleep after a painful hip problem robbed the proud dog of any mobility. She could hardly bear to let Hoot go because he was a living link to her son. By appearing with Hoot, Ethan let his mother know that they had both survived death and that she had made the right decision for Hoot.

One of the many wonderful things about pets is that they aren't critical about fashion choices and don't jeer when a game is lost due to a fumble. That makes them distinctly unlike peers. Peer pressure, on the other hand, can be fierce.

Peer to Peer

When my niece and nephew were growing up, I watched them with their friends. It was somewhat frightening how much influence friends and classmates had on fashion choices, games to play, music to listen to, and even vocabulary. There were times when I wasn't sure what language they were speaking because I couldn't understand a word.

Kids talk to kids, kids listen to kids . . . on earth and from heaven. Death doesn't seem to interrupt the interest that kids have in one another. This is a curious thing, though, from my standpoint as a medium.

For the most part, when people come to see me, they want to hear from very particular loved ones in spirit. These loved ones are often relatives or very close friends. On occasion, a not-so-close spirit stops in to say "hello," but there is usually a clear intent behind the visit. One such unusual circumstance comes to mind.

Several years ago, I was having a very enjoyable time with a woman named Betty and her family. In the midst of our visit, a spirit named May stopped in. Betty denied knowing her, but May insisted that she would soon understand. May's message was, "Tell my husband that I love him and I'm with him." I thanked May for coming even though Betty was puzzled by both her identity and her message.

Weeks later I received a call from Betty, who is a social worker. On the day following our meeting, she had an emergency appointment with a widower who was extremely distraught over the recent death of his wife. "I can't live without my May," he said. "I miss her so much. I want her to know how much I love her."

The only words that Betty could manage to say were, "Did you say that your wife's name was *May*?"

When the man said "yes," Betty faced a conundrum. As a social worker, she couldn't very well tell this man that his deceased wife had visited her during a session with a medium. What Betty did do, however, was strongly suggest that this bereaved husband visit the cemetery and tell his wife how much he loved and missed her. "I'm sure that May will hear you," Betty said with absolute confidence that she would. Betty also set him up with ongoing grief counseling.

A few days later, Betty received a call from May's husband. He felt much better after talking to his wife, he told her. He felt as though May was with him. When Betty related this story to me, she was very careful to protect the privacy of her client. May didn't have any such concerns; she wanted to get a message to her husband, saw an opportunity to get through, and took it.

Spirits are like that. They're opportunists—but in the best sense of the word. What astonishes me is how well organized all these communications seem to be. For the most part, random spirits don't just show up during sessions. With gazillions of people in the afterlife, matching specific spirits with their loved ones might seem like an impossible task. Fortunately, before someone comes to see me, their thoughts about the session arrive like e-mails in a heavenly in-box. The right recipients get the right message (for the most part).

Efforts at coordinating communication aren't only from our

side of death as discussed in chapter 2. The spirits make it their business to help set things up as well.

Years ago during a development circle, a group of helper spirits came to visit. One of the mediums in the group said, "They're telling me that they talk about you, Holli."

"Great," I said, "not only do I have to deal with the gossips in this world, they're gossiping in the next world, too."

"Oh no," the other medium said. "They discuss who to send to you." We all had a laugh about that. Nothing like having a heavenly booking agency.

I've experienced how the spirits run this booking agency. One woman who came to see me said, "A coworker told me about your work about a year ago. Then I got an e-mail from another medium and your name was mentioned in it. Just a month ago, as I was thinking about setting up an appointment with you, a girl walked by in a Hollister brand T-shirt. *That's it,* I thought. You're the medium I need to see."

When people tell me stories like this, I say, "Welcome to my world." The spirits send their loved ones to me, not necessarily because they think I'm the best medium in the world. It is usually because they know that my energy, talents, and personality will work well for their loved ones.

I say all this so that you understand that spirit communication isn't random, it is very directed. That's why it is even more interesting to me that kids in spirit speak with kids on earth despite the most tenuous connections. For a particular kid on earth to communicate with a kid in spirit, it's enough to have just been classmates, fellow camp buddies, neighbors, or just a friend of a friend. This point was made in a very dramatic way one night in Maryland a number of years ago.

A Cautionary Tale

"Is it okay for my grandson, Andrew, to join our family group tonight?" I was asked. Andrew, just shy of eighteen, had demonstrated an interest in spirit communication as well as a sensitivity to the spirits.

As a rule, I didn't permit people under eighteen to participate in sessions, events, and workshops at that time. The reason is very simple. Spirit communication is an energy-intensive endeavor and can be emotionally overwhelming, especially for younger participants. In recent years, however, I've met many younger people who are ready, willing, and very able to engage safely and happily with those living in the afterlife.

Andrew was one of those whom I felt was ready.

Our small group event took place in the warm family room of a gracious home. With the fireplace behind me, various family members seated comfortably in front of me, and counters laden with high-calorie snacks, we were ready to go.

A number of relatives in spirit stopped in to visit. Grandmothers, aunts, fathers-in-law, mothers-in-law, and favorite dogs visited with the group. After much laughter and sharing of memories, I noticed a girl in spirit who seemed to be roughly seventeen or eighteen. Her hair was long and blond. She was slight in build but determined in demeanor. She walked back and forth behind people relaxing on the tartan plaid sofa. They were oblivious to her presence, but once she knew that she had *my* attention, she started striding with purpose all the way around the group until she came to stand by Andrew.

"I don't know who she is," Andrew said when I described her to him.

The girl didn't falter; she stepped even closer to Andrew so that there would be no doubt that she was there for him. Then she started talking.

"I'm hearing a name that sounds like Christa, Crystal, or something like that," I told Andrew. "She's also giving me the names Jimmy and Tony. This girl passed in a car crash and she's insisting that you know about her. She's from another school, one that competes with your school in sports. She won't be graduating with her class this week."

As she kept talking, Andrew's eyes grew wider. "Jimmy and Tony are my best friends," he said. "Today we were talking about a girl from another school that they know. She died a couple of weeks ago, and won't be graduating with the rest of her class. Yeah, and our football team beat theirs."

"She's showing me two blinking lights, regular traffic lights that blink at night after a certain time. Do you know where these lights are?"

"No," Andrew answered.

"They're on your way home, she's telling me. Please be careful at the intersections where these lights are blinking."

Even though I'm sure that Andrew was thinking "big whoopin' deal" about the lights, he thought it was cool that someone his own age had come to say "hello."

After closing the circle, we descended upon the bountiful snacks. Talking to spirits always makes me hungry.

As I'm sure you know, this isn't the end of the story.

Several days later, I received a call from Andrew's grandmother. After staying late at her house talking about what happened at the group event, Andrew drove himself home. As he rounded a corner, he saw . . . a blinking traffic light. At the intersection, a police car with flashing lights was parked. There was a roadblock. After he answered a few questions, Andrew asked what was going on. He was told that there had been a murder at the recreation center down the street. The gunman was still at large. "Keep your car doors locked. Be careful," the policeman warned as Andrew drove off.

Andrew continued on his way, driving well below the limit with his headlights on bright, convinced that every moving shadow alongside the road was a man with a gun.

On one straight and long stretch of the deserted country road, he could see another blinking light in the distance. "Be careful." The officer's words echoed in his ear. He slowed the car, approaching the intersection with caution. Another police vehicle laid in wait at the blinking light. Andrew sat in his car waiting for the policeman to approach him. Instead of speaking with Andrew, however, the policeman grabbed a rifle and took off running across the field. Andrew found out later that shortly before he had reached the intersection, the suspect with the gun had been spotted on foot.

Although it is hard to say that if Andrew had been driving at the speed limit, his path would have intersected with that of a desperate gunman. It is reassuring, however, that a girl his own age took an interest in him and gave him a warning. One young girl in spirit and two blinking lights equals one *big* whoopin' deal in my mind.

During subsequent visits to the East Coast, Andrew attended other events. The girl with blond hair didn't come by again, but I know that her one and only visit made an impression on Andrew. It made an impression on me, too; and after all these years, I'm pretty hard to impress.

Intensive Care

Even kids who don't know each other at all on earth come to help one another when in spirit, especially if they've shared similar death experiences. Meeting a baby named Trevor demonstrated this in a way that I'll never forget.

Trevor's mother, Judith, called me for a session. When I told her that a little boy was there to see her, she enthusiastically told me that this was the reason for her call. The little boy used building blocks to spell out his name for me, which was very helpful. T-R-E-V-O-R appeared in blocks with red, orange, yellow, green, blue, and purple writing.

"He couldn't spell, though," Judith said.

"He says that you used to spell his name for him," I said in return.

"Yes, that's true," she replied. "I used to write out the letters of his name on his tummy."

"Trevor is showing me a bed that looks like a hospital bed to me. He says that he lived there," I told her. "He's showing me lots of tubes and I hear machines beeping."

There was silence on the line. "Are you there, Judith?" I asked.

"Yes," she said quietly.

"Trevor is showing me a scar on his chest from an operation. He's smiling, though, and laughing. He's holding up three fingers."

"I understand that," Judith whispered.

The room went silent. I could no longer hear the beeping of monitors. *Where did you go, Trevor?* I thought. *What happened to you?*

As though in an answer to my questions, my room filled

with blue light. I saw the hospital bed with a tiny body in it. Out of the body jumped a child, no more than a few months old. He stood by the bed for a moment with his mother by his side. Then he started to walk toward the door.

In my logical mind, I know that babies who are three months old can't walk. However, when the spirits are showing me a vision, I often have to leave behind how I think things have to be.

As Trevor walked toward the door, two little girls with pigtails entered to meet him. They took him by the hand and guided him through the doorway. As I followed these three little ones, I saw them join a long line of children walking down the hall of the hospital. There were boys and girls, babies, toddlers, and children. My thought was that it looked more like they were going on a school field trip than walking to heaven. Trevor waved and then was gone.

Once again I was aware of myself sitting in a chair with the phone in my hand. I didn't know how to begin to explain what I saw, so I started with a question. "Did Trevor die in a children's hospital?" I asked Judith.

"Yes," Judith said. "He was born with a severe heart defect. We had tried an operation while Trevor was in utero, but it didn't correct the problem entirely. He lived for three months in the hospital and died while I was sitting by his side."

"Oh Judith," I said, "your little boy was very well taken care of when he left his body. It seems to be that every child who died in that hospital came to walk him to heaven."

I could hear Judith sniffling. "Trevor's grandparents are all still alive," she said. "I was so worried that there would be no one to take care of him when he died. I was afraid that he would get lost."

When I shared the entire vision with Judith, the sound of her relief vibrated across the phone line.

That night when I went to bed, the room turned blue and I saw Trevor and his spirit friends again. This time, they all waved. And I waved back.

X-treme Supports

Kids in spirit stick together like kids on earth do. This is not to say that the afterlife is overrun by marauding groups of teen-agers who have abandoned their own families. Actually, the op-posite is true. Very often kids are banding together to *help* their families.

Innumerable times when meeting with a family that has a son and daughter in spirit, four, six, or even more kids in spirit will stand behind the one who is visiting the family. When this first started happening, I was a bit perturbed because I didn't understand why they were there en masse or to whom they all belonged. Even when the young person in spirit gave me names for those with him, I got blank looks from the parents in the room.

Then I got a call one day that helped to explain the phe-nomenon.

"Remember the kids you mentioned when we met with you?" the woman on the phone asked me.

"I remember that you didn't know what I was talking about!" I responded.

She laughed in a way that bordered on a giggle. "I know what our son Benjamin was doing," she said. "The day after we met with you, my husband and I attended our first grief support meeting. When the others in the room started talking about their children, some of the names you gave us were mentioned. Benjamin was visiting us with the kids belonging to the people in our group. We didn't know their names because we hadn't met their parents yet."

She also mentioned that when her husband, who was not only a skeptic about mediumship but was also wary of attending a support group, couldn't explain what had happened as simply mind reading or coincidence, he agreed to continue going to the support group meetings so he could solve the puzzle.

"That's just like our Benjamin," she said. "My husband thinks that he's the one figuring things out, but it's Benjamin who figured out how to get his father to keep going to the group meetings."

Kids in spirit are not only smart and wise, but they are doing whatever they can to help their parents get the help and healing support they need to come to terms with death. Kids not only want their parents to learn how to live again, but they want to learn the best ways to communicate *directly* with their parents too.

When I'm talking with a kid in spirit—especially with a teenager—I feel as though I'm being practiced on. Although I may be focusing my attention on one spirit, I can also sense the attention of others in the group. It's as if I'm being watched. During most sessions, spirits will try to use my heightened senses to get their messages across. But kids in spirit are aggressive this way—they will play with *all* of my senses. I'll see something, then hear something, then feel something, then taste something. By contrast, when I work with adults in spirit, they tend to use only one sense. Often, it is my "hearing." Or in the event that a person wasn't a big conversationalist while on earth, he or she may choose to communicate with me in pictures.

So naturally, when I'm in a session with a group of kids in spirit, I often hear chatter and laughter in the background as information starts coming to me in lots of different ways. I'll see an image, then hear a name, then feel the personality of the teenager in spirit, then perhaps smell a cake baking, or a sweaty locker room. I joked with one mother by saying, "Your son and the kids he's with are pushing all my buttons!" The mother replied, "When he was little, our son loved to push all the buttons in the elevator so that we had to stop at every floor." Her son was still pushing all the buttons, only in spirit he was learning precisely which buttons to push to get an odor noticed, a sound heard, an image seen or to get across a sense of his personality. And he was teaching other kids how to do it too!

Groups of kids in spirit are like students graduating with a master's in communication from Afterlife U. Their group intent, which can sometimes feel very intense for the medium, is to learn the most effective ways to let their families know that they are alive and well and still very much around. Once kids figure out how to get through, they can be very enthusiastic communicators. When I was doing an event for about sixty grieving parents, a young man in spirit caught my eye by jumping up and down and waving his arms as though he was at a ball game. I could hear cheering in the background from the other kids in the room, when I first noticed him. It was almost as though, in that moment, spirit communication became a team sport.

Pushing Limits

Once in a while, kids in spirit can become so enthusiastic that encounters get physical.

"I've been goosed!" I exclaimed.

"Someone just grabbed my breasts," squealed my friend Michelle, who was sitting next to me.

First of all, let me make it clear that these are not the usual antics of spirits I meet with every day. This interactive experience happened during one of my weekly development circles. Six of us were gathered in a darkened room as usual. After our prayers of blessing and requests for protection, we heard sounds as though the furniture in the room was being moved. We could hear the stones and crystals on a table rattling as though someone was tossing them into a bag.

As things got noisier, several people in the group got the impression that two boys in spirit were present. They seemed to be in their mid teens. These boys weren't dressed in modern-day clothing but looked to be from the 1950s. When I asked them what they were doing, one asked questions in return. "You can hear us? You can feel us touching you?" We answered "yes" in unison.

Our reactions must have greatly encouraged the boys because before long, we heard the table in the center of our circle start to rock back and forth. "Why are you pushing things around?" I asked them.

"To see if we can," one replied. They could, and they did. Sitting on the table in the center of our circle was a round item resting on a piece of paper. We had outlined the item on the piece of paper beneath it. We did this as an informal test so that we could see if the item moved during our time in the dark. When we ended the circle, the object was knocked out of the outline we had drawn. The furniture in the room and other articles were still in place and nothing had been damaged, but there had indeed been movement and the tracings on the paper indicated this.

I'd like to stress again that this is not a usual occurrence, but it does illustrate that when together, kids like to make an impact and discover ways in which their presence can be known, even if those ways are spectacular or peculiar. They seem to be learning as much as those of us in our development circle were.

During another small group event, several young people in spirit not only made an impact but also demonstrated their determination to change the lives of their peers. Here's their story.

Divine Intervention

It was the perfect sunny California day. As usual, I was rushing around trying to get things ready for the ten people who were coming in hopes of hearing from loved ones in spirit.

After the room was straightened, the chairs arranged, and the ice water set out on the table, I sat quietly and asked the spirits to use my talents to help bring healing and loving change to those attending the event.

As the group gathered, I noticed a friendly, personable young couple in their late twenties settle in between two other couples in their late forties or so. They were the youngest people in the room—until the spirits showed up, that is.

After ending the opening prayer, I lifted my eyes and saw a stunning sight. Standing behind the young man was a line of young men in spirit extending beyond the walls of the room. Their facial features were indistinct, and as I glanced toward the end of the line, their outlines became mere shadows. I stared at them and they stared back at me. I could feel their gaze even though I couldn't see their eyes.

"What are you doing here?" I asked the group in my mind. The entire group spoke with one voice as though they were a Greek chorus.

"We're here for him. We're here because of him. We're here to help him."

Although I didn't know what to make of this, I started giving the information to the young man sitting in front of me. The spirits, however, stopped me mid sentence to make the reason for their coming very clear. The young men standing in my living room were dead *because* of the actions of the young man sitting in my living room.

I still didn't understand how that could be possible, but I passed along the information as I am bound to do. "These young men standing behind you are telling me that they're dead because of you."

He looked at me with eyes that seemed to mirror the sorrow of the world.

"I know why," he said. "I was in a gang."

The two middle-aged couples sitting near him shifted in their seats. So did I.

There was nothing about the young man sitting before me that said "gang." Okay, so maybe his clothes were a little baggy. But there were no tattoos that I could see and he looked anything *but* menacing.

Just as these thoughts were dashing through my head, a man in spirit appeared next to the young man. He gave me the feeling of being a father; and the information started pouring into me.

"Your father is here," I said. "He is a tall, imposing man with a military background. He's standing in a uniform, looks like army to me."

"Yeah, my father was in the army," the young man acknowledged.

"Your father is writing three letters in the sky before my eyes, G-E-D. He gives me the feeling that he helped you with that. He's proud of you for making something of your life." As I finished that last statement the young man's eyes brimmed with tears.

"I got my GED in jail *after* he died. How could he know about it?" he asked after clearing his throat.

"After someone dies, he can still be aware of what is happening here on earth and in the lives of those left behind," I explained.

With the back of his hand, the young man roughly wiped away his tears.

"I thought I had disappointed my father in *every* way," he said, his voice thick with the tears he had tried to wipe away. "When I got my GED, I didn't think that he would ever know."

In that moment, this young man's perspective shifted. With sudden confidence, he sat up straighter in his chair.

His father wasn't finished, however. "Your father and the boys [he indicated the young men standing in line] are going to help you to help others and change lives. You will be speaking to groups, going to prisons and places like that."

I paused to take a breath. The young man looked at me, surprised.

"Just last week I met with some people who want me to speak to groups about my life. I'm thinkin' about it, but I'm scared to talk in front of people. I feel kinda pushed to do it anyway."

After seeing all those young men standing behind him, I had no doubt why he was feeling pushed. *How could someone who had been jailed for gang activity be afraid to talk in front of a group anyway?* I asked myself.

The boys in line had one last thing to say before they would let me move on.

"We're connected," they said. Then the Greek chorus fell silent and the young men and the father vanished before my eyes.

In the silence that followed this message, we passed around tissues. Having a gang member in our midst probably should have been terrifying. Instead, as a group, we were all touched by the love of a father proud of his son, the grace of the young men who had died by violence, and the determination of the young man who had resolved to make a difference in his life.

To this day, I get emotional when I think about this encounter. Wherever prejudice, hate, and death separate us one from another, kids in spirit remind us that despite any perceived differences, we *are* all connected. Kids in spirit join their peers on earth to create new beginnings even out of devastating destruction. No matter how terrible things may look, there is a lot more going on behind the scenes than we can imagine. Kids in spirit are busy making an impact on earth and joined with their peers here, they are creating a future for all of us to share.

Spirit ANSWERS

Do only the good die young?

Fortunately not, but it makes a great song lyric. Whenever a wonderful child or a talented, kind young adult dies, it may be natural to assume that they were so good that they no longer needed to be here on earth to learn anything. However, I've met some amazingly wonderful spirits who lived to a very ripe old age. This world would be unlivable if all the good people died young. Many exemplary people who live in service to others, like Gandhi and Mother Teresa, have died late in life.

From the perspective of the spirits, the most important thing about their life and death is not how long they lived on earth or even how they died. It is how they have loved.

Is there peer pressure in the afterlife?

Certainly not in the way that we experience it on earth! While growing up, kids may dress and behave in order to be accepted as part of a group. Being considered an outsider or "uncool" must be avoided at all costs. As a result, teenagers may be willing to risk embarrassment and even death by taking part in behavior like indiscriminate sex, underage drinking, and street racing. However, in the afterlife, spirits aren't categorized according to the demographics we're familiar with on earth. Spirits aren't separated by age, race, or education, as geeks or as cool people. Instead, peers in spirit are of like mind and heart. I've been told by some spirits that, in the afterlife, there is a real sense of belonging, of being part of a greater whole, while at the same time retaining the imprints of their lives on earth. When a teenager in spirit showed me his purple hair and piercings, he was using these distinctive "identifiers" to say to his siblings and parents, "Hey, it's me." This doesn't mean, however, that he is hanging out with punk rockers in the afterlife. Instead, this particular boy wanted his mother to know that he was with her brother, who had died in a similar manner twenty years before.

Do spirits band together in groups? Do they form gangs in the afterlife?

When speaking with a mother, I said, "Your son, Chase, is giving me the sense that he was a leader at school. I'm seeing posters and flyers that say 'Class President.' Chase is surrounded by kids in spirit who want to make a difference in this world." "Oh, yes," Chase's mom replied. "He was elected class president and he ran with the slogan, "Make a Difference." Chase went on to communicate his interest in human rights here on earth and told his mother that he and his friends in spirit were inspiring a friend of hers to raise money to build schools overseas. "That's my Chase," she said. During numerous instances, kids in spirit (and grown people, too) have indicated to me that they were working toward change on earth and joining with others in spirit (and on earth) to accomplish these goals.

So, whenever I see on the news that there is a spontaneous outpouring of aid to people in need, or a sudden, unexplained inspiration that leads to a medical breakthrough, I can't help but think that there are spirits like Chase banding together with other spirits on his side of life to help us on this side.

Do kids meet and make new friends with other kids in spirit?

Kids in spirit often bring new friends in spirit to sessions with family members on earth. These are friends they met for the first time in the afterlife. They also mention seeing friends of friends or friends of the family who have recently passed. One of the more astonishing things I've witnessed are groups of kids arriving together to a session because their parents are linked in some loose way. For example, kids whose parents are attending a support group or raising money for the same charity may appear together. These kids have rarely met or known one another while on earth. In almost every instance there is purpose in their meeting, and that purpose is usually to provide loving support to their families.

How do spirits have fun?

My great aunt Day used to say, "Life is just so damned daily." I think that many people would agree with her. Fun is what distracts us from the concerns of everyday living. However, in the afterlife the routines of physical life don't necessarily exist. There are no nine-to-five jobs per se or chores like doing the laundry on Saturdays. People can enjoy what they like about life. They can relish beautiful gardens without ever having to weed or mow the grass.

"Fun" is also what we call experiences shared with those we love. Taking vacations, visiting theme parks, and sailing along a great river qualify as fun because we're laughing with friends and family members. Fun is what constitutes some of our best memories.

Dying doesn't make these memories disappear. In the afterlife, spirits readily recall the moments of love they shared amidst all the fun. During sessions, they'll mention vacations, barbecues, family reunions, and other such times. However, in the afterlife, the notion of "fun" is replaced by the experience and the magnificence of a joy beyond anything we can imagine, a peace that extends beyond our understanding, and perfected love.

Spirit SUMMARY

Kids in spirit experience the feeling of belonging, of being part of a group without any of the destructive aspects of peer pressure that exist here on earth. Because kids in spirit understand the challenges facing the young, they encourage and inspire their peers on earth in surprising and original ways, even those they may not have known before. The grief, needs, and concerns of their parents also bring kids in spirit together to help them provide the support their parents often need to go on with day-to-day living.

8

Over Before It Started

Aborted, Miscarried, and Stillborn Children Speak

$\mathcal{S}pirit$ TWEET

"In one breath you gave me enough love for a lifetime."
(Spoken by a baby who died in her father's arms.)

$\mathcal{S}pirit$ THOUGHTS

Pregnant Pauses

Kirsten made a frantic hand gesture, which I interpreted to mean *"Shut off the recorder!"* So I did.

"My husband doesn't know that I had an abortion," she explained in her slight foreign accent. "So I can't have that on the tape." I nodded and set the recorder aside.

"As your mother was saying," I continued as though nothing untoward had happened, "she is here with your baby, the one that was aborted."

"Oh, God, I didn't know what to do," said Kirsten, as she began to cry. "My husband and I were separated at the time. I didn't want to bring a baby into our mess so I *had* to have an *abortion.*" Kirsten spit out the word "abortion" as though it was poison on her tongue. Her eyes darted back and forth looking for escape. The abortion was a secret that Kirsten had obviously never intended to share with *anyone.* Well, the spirits had a different plan.

Kirsten's unleashed emotional reaction surprised me. Up until that point she had been completely composed despite the chilling story her parents in spirit had to tell.

Kirsten's father had described his murder by a gang of thieves while tending to his ranch on another continent. Kirsten's mother, also no match for the intruders, did her best to alert the authorities by activating an alarm wired to the nearest police station. When the officers arrived, Kirsten's mother was dead as well, her hand having left a bloody print on the wall by the alarm's panic button. Kirsten was able to converse with both of her parents during our session, showing little or no emotion, each strand of upswept blond hair remaining perfectly in place throughout. However, when it came to the subject of abortion, she was far more easily upset. In fact, she had become completely undone.

Kirsten's mother took no notice of her distress and continued with her messages.

"Your mother is telling me that she and your baby in spirit were with you when you bought a wooden toy chest for the twins last week. Your baby likes being around the twins and watching out for them."

Kirsten's panicked face softened slightly. "I thought about my baby while buying that chest."

"There is an elephant painted on the front, isn't there?"

"Why yes," Kirsten replied, surprised. She paused and I could tell that she wanted to ask a question, one that was difficult to voice. "My baby really isn't dead?" she asked after clearing her throat several times.

"Your baby is alive and with your mother," I assured her.

"Was it a boy or a girl?" she asked.

"I really don't know. Neither the baby in spirit nor your mother is telling me that," I responded.

"I always wanted a girl," Kirsten said wistfully.

Regret. Anxiety. Guilt. Shame. Almost always, women express one or more of these emotions when a spirit who passed with abortion is present, even among women who maintain a belief in choice. These spirits might be expected to respond with anger, confusion, hurt, and feelings of rejection . . . but they don't. Instead, they shine. And I mean this literally.

Spirits who haven't lived long enough to walk on earth have a particular way of announcing their presence to me; they appear as little twinkling stars or light, usually above the left shoulder of the woman who either had an abortion or a miscarriage. These spirits may also appear in the arms of a family member or friend, but that usually occurs when a specific incident around the pregnancy is being highlighted, such as a late-term abortion due to medical complications or a late-term miscarriage.

In some cases where an abortion has taken place, the spirit will send me a few thoughts that are specifically related to what was going on at the time the abortion took place. Sometimes I may even get a sense of whether their energy is masculine or feminine, but most times neither their gender nor their personality are discernible to me.

Generally, the spirits I work with provide specific personal characteristics and information that can be confirmed by the sitter or the sitter's family and friends. In speaking with a spirit who has been aborted, however, there are no such frames of reference. Instead, relatives in spirit often speak for them.

This is true because those who have passed through abortion did not yet have fully formed bodies. Therefore, they don't have attachments to the idea of a physical being at all. Spirits are ageless and are only subject to the characteristics of aging when they are in a physical body.

In many instances, a spirit is more willing to mention abortion than a woman is willing to admit to it.

"No, no, I don't know what you're talking about," the woman with striking good looks said. She stared me directly in the eyes as she denied knowledge of such a child in the presence of a larger group.

"Well, I don't know what to tell you," I replied. "Your friend, Joe, says that he is here with your baby, the one that passed with abortion. I'm seeing a sparkle of light above your shoulder, which means that the baby in spirit is here."

"I know nothing about an abortion," she protested again, folding her arms across her chest.

In situations like this I know what I'm seeing and I know what I'm hearing, but I also know when to quit. I am less concerned about appearing to be correct than I am about faithfully delivering the message. Once I've delivered the message, I figure that I'm finished. Joe, however, didn't agree. *He* wasn't finished.

"Your friend Joe says that the two of you had no secrets when he was alive," I relayed.

"That's true," she said. "We told each other everything."

"Not everything, he's saying. There was one secret he found out about after he died."

"Okay, okay, I get it," she said.

Then I moved on.

During the break halfway through the event, I was trying to eat a piece of cheesecake when the striking woman pulled me aside. "I want to let you know that you were right about the abortion."

"Mmm . . . mmm," I said, my mouth full of creamy goodness.

"I just didn't want the other ladies to know. You know how it is, a small town and all," she explained.

I nodded and kept chewing. Even if this lovely but conflicted lady thought that I would challenge her decision, I couldn't have gotten a word out with a mouth full of food.

As a medium, I am not a judge; I am a communicator. I work with the spirits from a loving and balanced perspective, a place where forgiveness is a path to freedom and the goal is healing broken relationships beyond death. The place from which I work is best described by the mystical thirteenth-century Persian poet Rumi:

Out beyond ideas of wrongdoing and rightdoing,
There is a field. I'll meet you there.
When the soul lies down in that grass,
The world is too full to talk about.
Ideas, language, even the phrase *each other*
doesn't make any sense.

–From *Essential Rumi* by Coleman Barks

It is doubtful that the spirit named Joe was a Rumi fan, but he sure wasn't concerned about who in the group might judge his friend. He was concerned about a secret that caused separation and shame. This lady whom he loved had held out on him, and he wasn't having any of it!

Joe was the spirit's representative, as is often the case. Abortions don't go unnoticed by friends and relatives in the afterlife. They want to share the secret because in sharing it, healing begins.

More than once in my experience, the twinkling spirit of an aborted baby serves as a catalyst for healing. When the light of these spirits appears in my sessions, it is often in relation to concerns about a history of damaging behavior that friends and family in spirit wish to address.

One mother in spirit told her daughter how excited she was that she was getting married and planned to start a family right away. "I love babies," the mother declared and at that moment I saw three twinkling lights. The mother told her daughter not to worry, that she *would* be able to have children. I thought that this statement was odd considering that I could see three aborted spirits in this young woman's past. She obviously had no trouble getting pregnant!

"I was wild growing up," the girl confided. "One of the reasons I'm here today is to be sure that my mom knows that I've straightened out. I was worried that I might be punished for having abortions—that maybe I'd already used up my chances to have a baby."

It was then that her mother told her of a botched illegal abortion that she had had before being married. She, too, had been afraid that she would never be able to have a child. (The illegal abortion was later confirmed by the young woman's aunt.)

The twinkling spirits of the aborted babies prompted these two women to share mutual experiences and anxieties that up to this point had remained hidden from each other.

The spirit lights of aborted babies, as small as they may seem individually, collectively illuminate the deepest and darkest corners of fear. Wherever there is the fear of being found out, the lights of their spirits shine. Wherever there is guilt, shame, and regret, their silent lights can help to illuminate the way back to peace.

Infant-ite Wisdom

Up to this point our discussion of babies in spirit has represented the woman's choice of whether or not to have the baby. But there *is* a different point of view to consider. In some cases, it is the baby who decides to be born . . . or not. To stay on earth . . . or not.

"There's a little girl dancing in circles around you," I said to the woman sitting in the center of a small group. "She tells me that she is six years old."

"I lost my baby, but she wasn't six when she died," the woman responded. She huffed a bit and settled back into her chair, seemingly relieved that the spotlight wasn't going to remain on her.

"She's telling me that she's six now," I responded. "You've just celebrated her birthday."

After hesitating, the woman spoke. "My baby would have been six yesterday. My baby would have been six. My ba-ba-baby . . ." The rest of her words were lost in sobs and she sat there crumpled like a piece of paper in a giant's hand.

At moments like these, it would be easy to start sobbing

myself. It is natural to respond with empathy and attempt to comfort someone so obviously devastated and broken by grief. As harsh as it may sound, though, I can't get caught up in emotions when I'm talking with spirits. Through experience I know that a personal emotional response can interfere or even stop the flow of messages from coming through altogether. My emphasis and focus has to remain on giving the spirits a voice in the conversation even if I seem unsympathetic to the rest of the people present.

Something just occurred to me while writing about emotion just now. Oddly enough, in all the years I've been speaking with spirits, I've never heard a baby cry in spirit or a child whine. Not once. There is laughter, plenty of giggles and smiles, but no tears. Weeping and crying are *our* expressions of separation, desperation, frustration, and need here on earth. Babies and kids in spirit live in peace, abundance, and above all, joy. There is no need for tears. There is no hunger in the afterlife. There are no lost toys in in the afterlife.

Adults in spirit may express regret or disappointment for their actions on earth, but even they don't stand there crying when they talk to me. Spirits deal with their faults in a straightforward way, for the most part. One of my mother's favorite sayings was, "No use crying over spilled milk." Apparently, there's no place where that is truer than in in the afterlife.

However, right in front of me that night there were enough tears to overflow the banks of earth and flood the afterlife completely. People sitting next to the sobbing woman touched her arms to comfort her. Wads of tissues appeared to supplement those falling to the floor.

"Your child, who is now six, is telling me that she wasn't sick before she died. She's showing me a beautiful pink bed with a baby in it who, I think, is about eighteen months old. She's big for her age, she's telling me. When she was a baby, she liked to watch Mickey Mouse spinning over her head."

The woman nodded.

"She died in that bed, she's telling me. She was sleeping and didn't wake up. She gives me a name that sounds like Cassie."

The woman nodded again.

"She wants you to know that she didn't leave because she doesn't love you. Your baby girl loves you. She's showing me a bracelet with letters on it. You have that with you, right?"

Mutely, the woman pulled a tiny bracelet out of her pocket.

"You had to request that the bracelet be returned to you, didn't you?" I asked. "Your baby girl is telling me that there was an investigation, but that you did nothing wrong. She keeps repeating over and over that you did nothing wrong!" I said with emphasis.

"Then why did she leave me?" the lady asked through her sobs.

I paused for a moment waiting for an answer. Instead of words, this precious six-year-old showed me a movie in my head of a little girl growing up too fast, outgrowing her clothes, outgrowing her bed, and outgrowing her house. It was a bit like watching a scene from *Alice in Wonderland*.

"I used to read that story to her," the grieved mother said, momentarily tear-free. "She grew so fast. I had to buy new clothes for her every week. It's like she was too big for her body and just grew out of it," she finished with a sigh.

I wasn't sure if Cassie's mother realized the broader implications of what she was saying, but I did. Other kids had told me that their bodies could no longer contain their spirits. After her mother's statement, Cassie began dancing again as though in agreement. When I mentioned this, her mother said, "Yesterday for her birthday, I put on some music and danced around. I told my baby that I couldn't stop celebrating the day she came into my life."

"She's still dancing with you," I said. "As far as she's concerned, the party isn't over."

During a break halfway through the event, Cassie's mother shared her story with me. Cassie had been a big baby, weighing in at over ten pounds. Her pink bed still had the Mickey Mouse mobile hanging over it. One day while taking a nap, Cassie died. Just like that. Cassie's father, who was estranged from her mother, made accusations of child neglect and abuse. During the subsequent investigation, nothing was found to support his claims and Cassie's death was ascribed to SIDS (sudden infant death syndrome). Despite being exonerated, Cassie's mother had blamed herself. Four years of tears came pouring forth that night, but Cassie, the little girl whose spirit outgrew her body, ended the evening with a dance.

Looking Good for Your Age

Cassie wasn't the first spirit I had met who showed me that a spirit doesn't have to appear as the age at which they died. Many people who have died in their seventies, eighties, and nineties appear during a session at a fit forty. Fortunately, they tend to present themselves in a form familiar to their loved ones and then later present the form they had during the time they were happiest and healthiest. When one debonair father in spirit showed himself all spiffed up with a full head of hair leaning jauntily on a sports car, his daughter laughed and said, "Dad was hot stuff in those days." When people in spirit come to visit, they'll often show themselves "spiffed up."

For babies in spirit, however, the opposite seems to be true. Babies don't usually appear younger. Oftentimes they appear *older* than they were when they died, as in Cassie's case. Babies haven't had a lifetime of becoming attached to or identified with a particular body and are extremely changeable in the way that they choose to present themselves to me.

Sometimes a miscarried baby can appear as an older companion to another child in spirit, especially if they're siblings. Recently when meeting with a mother, I mentioned that her teenage son in spirit was walking along the beach with another boy. "He's telling me that the boy he's with is his brother." The lovely lady gasped and said, "Before my son was born, I had a miscarriage. I always thought it was a boy and told my son that he had an older brother. Whenever we went to the beach, we imagined that my other son was with us. I'm glad that they're together enjoying the beach in the afterlife."

One miscarriage can be disheartening for people yearning to be parents, a series of miscarriages absolutely devastating. For one woman, though, her desire to be a parent had unexpected results.

A Heavenly Birthday Party

Maggie sat perfectly composed, auburn hair drawn back in a ponytail, horn-rimmed glasses highlighting her sky blue eyes. She was the epitome of what I assumed a preschool teacher would look like. The children gathering at her feet were various ages, from infants to kindergarteners. As they sat down around her, it looked as though they were getting ready for story time. *What a perfect picture*, I thought. Except Maggie wasn't a preschool teacher and the well-behaved children at Maggie's feet were spirits.

"You're surrounded by children, young ones," I told Maggie. "They're very well behaved."

"Yes, I understand," Maggie said. I'm glad that she understood, because I didn't.

"They're each saying the word 'joy' to me," I continued, "but I don't know if that is one of their names. I'm hearing 'joy, joy, joy.'"

With that, Maggie smiled and said, "I know who you're talking to. I'd better explain." (I must have looked puzzled.) "I've been trying for years to have a baby. All my pregnancies ended in miscarriages. I call them my 'little joys.'"

I didn't know what to say. Most of the parents I meet who have lost children don't seem nearly as relaxed and accepting.

"Your little joys are telling me that there's another little joy at home waiting for you, a baby boy with an 'R' name."

"Yes," she said with a smile. "I was finally able to bring a baby to term. His name is Russ and he's six months old now," she said, beaming. "I came here tonight to be sure that *all* my babies know that I love them. Now I know more than that. I know that all of them are with me."

Joy Comes in Small Packages

Joy is one of the things babies bring into our lives. The irrepressible delight that bubbles out of them is absolutely infectious. When a baby laughs, it is almost impossible not to laugh in response. My mother was the quintessential lover of little ones and I think that because of her influence, joy, fun, and laughter have always been a big part of my life. When I first started working with the spirits, I was stunned to find out that joy isn't as bountiful in all families. Last year, I was dismayed to discover that one of my dearest friends had never experienced sheer joyful abandon. But one little girl in spirit was about to show her how.

> Ring around the rosy
> A pocket full of posies
> Ashes, ashes
> We all fall down!

I lay in bed, not wanting to open my eyes. Who needs an alarm clock, when a little girl in spirit decides to sing in the morning?

This spirit introduced herself as Daisy and only after my morning cup of coffee was I able to admit that she was a charming and joyous presence.

Also at breakfast I learned that Daisy was the daughter my friend Janet had unwittingly miscarried due to an IUD failure.

I had visited with Janet and stayed at her home for several years before ever meeting Daisy. This isn't as surprising as it sounds. Spirits sometimes wait decades to make their presence known. But even with such delays, their timing is always perfect. It's as if they instinctively know when we're ready for their messages, which isn't always when we think we are.

Another reason for Daisy's delayed visit may have had something to do with the years Janet spent preparing herself for spirit communication. Janet's interest began casually as she read books and took development workshops and classes in metaphysics. Then it intensified as she began surrounding herself with other people sensitive to spirits (I am just one of those people, by the way). In time, Janet's own natural sensitivity became more refined. Daisy clearly waited until Janet was ready to fully receive her messages.

Janet is a retired schoolteacher who never married. Her passion for learning and her offbeat sense of humor, which is a lot like mine, have made us easy friends. Her love for spirit communication is a bonus.

Daisy also possesses a unique brand of humor. One day during my stay I was conducting a group event. As I was trying to concentrate on providing messages to a lovely family who had lost their patriarch and a son, I was distracted by two children playing hide-and-seek around the sofa. One of these children was, of course, the very impish Daisy.

Once Daisy knew that I could see her, she wreacked all sorts of havoc, which continued well after the event. Even Janet's dog, Calla, ran from her playful antics.

I was thrown by the commotion. *This has to stop*, I thought at first. *This little girl doesn't realize the effect she's having on the people (and animals) she's around.* I was taking my job as spirit nanny very seriously, until it occurred to me that maybe she did know the effect she was having after all. Let me explain.

During the years I've known Janet, we've had many sessions together. So many fruitful ones, in fact, that I had long given up worrying that there might not be anything left for the spirits to talk about. Whenever the spirits visit Janet, they always bring along another visitor or two from her extensive family tree. In fact, a spirit from the 1600s once showed up during a phone session. As it turned out, Janet had been researching that branch of the family just the week before.

One of the reasons I greatly enjoy meeting with people and their spirits over time is that I get to witness the changes in their lives. These changes are often the result of the mending of relationships that were broken by unloving behaviors on earth.

In Janet's life, her relationship with her father had been severely damaged due to his alcoholism. (Yes, this is a more common theme in life than you may realize!) Through sessions with me and other mediums, Janet and her father had finally reconciled their differences. Through forgiveness, the traumas of the past began to lose their hold over the present. As a result of this healing, Janet was ready for the next phase of her growth.

Enter Daisy.

Well into my session with Janet, Daisy started to talk about all the fun things she had wanted to do with us during the few days of R&R we had planned at Janet's beach cottage. She mentioned popcorn among the snacks she wanted to eat at the boardwalk. (I was happy to comply with that request.) It wasn't long before Daisy got into the real reason for her interest in Janet.

"There will be more children brought to you, she's telling me. She's excited about that. Have you ever thought about writing children's books about the other side?" I asked, being prompted by Daisy.

"Well, people want me to," Janet replied. "I've thought of it, but I don't necessarily have a drive to do it."

"Daisy says that the drive is going to come from joy. But first you have to have joy in your life to understand the joy of children. She says that this is part of the reason why she and the other children in spirit will be in your life."

Daisy was talking fast. I had to take a quick breath so that I could keep up with her.

"I feel like Daisy may sometimes show herself to you as older, or even younger. She will show you herself going through different stages of life."

"Yes, a couple of other mediums have seen her do that. They saw her morph into a young woman," Janet said.

"She needs you to see how elastic she can be. She says that you can be the same way. Just because you are at a certain stage in your life doesn't mean that you can't also be a little girl running through the field and picking flowers without a care in the world. The two of you can be children together."

"She's asked me to play dollies with her," Janet said.

"Her presence in your life is about having joy in your life. In many ways, it is about reclaiming your own childhood."

Janet agreed with Daisy's assessment of the situation.

In thinking about the meeting with Daisy and Janet, I was struck by Daisy's determination—and her wisdom. She had lived for two months in Janet's womb before the IUD kicked her out. But that wasn't going to stop her from becoming a real presence in Janet's life. In some ways, their journey together was just beginning.

Later that night while we were eating ice cream, I asked Janet if she had ever had joy in her life.

"No," she said laconically. "With Daddy's drinking, we literally lost the farm. Any hope of an idyllic childhood escaped me on that day."

But according to Daisy, hope had not been lost at all. Babies in spirit remind us that we can experience the joy of childhood, even if we never had it in the first place. We can effectively reclaim what may have been withheld due to the actions of others. New joy is a gift that babies in spirit give us here on earth. Daisy was determined to help Janet capture that joy. And writing fantastical and magical children's stories seemed like a very good place to start.

Love is a precious gift that babies bring into our lives. Even babies in spirit are capable of delivering it to us in abundance. The number of months or years they've spent with us here on earth is immaterial; their love knows no bounds in measure or timing. I learned this lesson from Daisy, as well as from another dear little girl who visited with her father one night at an event I was conducting in West Hollywood, California, several years later.

One-of-a-Kind Love

As I looked out over the audience, a speeding blur circling the first and second rows caught my eye. *Slow down,* I said in my head, *I can't see you.*

In response, the blur came into greater focus and I could finally begin to make out the figure of a young girl who was about four years old. Once she knew that I could see her, she ran behind a man in the front row and hid.

This won't do, I said in my mind, while giving introductory remarks to the crowd. In response, she peeked out from behind his chair.

"There's a little girl standing behind you," I said to the man in the front row. "You have a daughter in spirit?"

"Yes."

"She loves to run," I said. "She likes running with you every morning."

"How do you know that I run every morning?" he asked me, with a bit of an edge in his voice.

"I know because she's telling me," I responded. "I don't know where you live and certainly don't have the time to spy on you!"

"I was surprised that you said that, that's all," he explained with a little less edge.

"This is an athletic little girl," I continued. "She says that you wanted a boy, but that was okay. She wanted to play football for your college team anyway!"

He laughed and seemed to relax a bit more. "When my wife got pregnant, I told her that our son was going to be the star running back at my alma mater, like I was."

Now it was the little girl's turn to laugh. "I was a girl instead. I was Daddy's little girl. I'm special." In my mind's eye, she showed me a bedroom all in pink, with stuffed animals everywhere and a unicorn in the crib.

"Before she was born, my wife and I bought the unicorn for her so that she would know that she is unique, one of a kind," he said while indicating a lovely brunette woman sitting next to him.

Although I found it unusual that the little girl hadn't acknowledged her mother, I trusted that she knew what she was doing.

"She's giving me the name Alice or Allison, and says that she enjoyed playing with her cousins at the family get-together at the lake."

"Her name *is* Allison. We recently had a family reunion at the lake where our family spent summers when I was young," Allison's father said. "My sister had a baby girl right about the time that Allison was born, so they would have been the same age."

Then all the running, hiding, and seeking came to an end. Little Allison the four-year-old became a baby in front of my eyes. I didn't know what to make of this sudden shift in body size.

"I don't understand why she is doing this," I admitted. "But Allison is showing herself to me as a baby. She shows herself being held by you." I pointed to her father. "While you're holding her she says, 'Daddy, in one breath you gave me enough love for a lifetime.'"

At that moment, Allison's daddy covered his face with his hands. He leaned forward and for a moment I thought that he would fall. His wife gently stroked his back, ignoring her own tears. After a shuddering breath, Allison's daddy began to speak through his hands.

"If Allison had lived, she would be four years old today," he began. "As soon as she was born, I held her in my arms." He paused, dropped his hands from his face, squared his jaw and said, "When I held her in my arms, she took one breath . . . and died."

Allison, once again appearing as though she had lived to be four years old, urged me to repeat her words.

"Daddy, in one breath you gave me enough love for a lifetime."

Spirit ANSWERS

Do miscarried or aborted children wait in the afterlife to unite with their would-be parents?

Although I can't say yes for sure, all my experiences with those who were almost born lead me to conclude that, in spirit, they remain with their intended families. This conclusion is supported by many individual examples. Here are two that illustrate the point.

Once I met with a woman named Kimberly. I also met her daughter in spirit, who had died in a miscarriage. Although she had died in the womb, this baby was delivered normally, and Kimberly even gave her a name, Ava. Kimberly had always wanted to give birth to a little girl, and in a manner of speaking, she had. In my session, Ava mentioned that her mother prayed for her every day. Kimberly confirmed this, also adding that Ava had been buried in the family plot. In this case, Kimberly and Ava had a mother/daughter bond that transcended birth . . . and death. Kimberly expressed a desire to be with Ava when she got to heaven. Ava agreed to always stay by Kimberly's side, which may mean that they will be united in the afterlife. Ava didn't give me even the slightest indication that she was interested in looking for another family.

A similar message came through in a session I had with a woman named Nicole from San Diego. When Nicole's miscarried baby girl appeared during the session, she mentioned that her mother talks to her every day. The baby even mentioned that Nicole has seen her and that she watches out for her little brother. Nicole confirmed that after her son was born, she saw a little spirit girl peeking into her son's bassinet. She felt that this was her miscarried daughter. From that day forward she talked to her daughter in spirit and included her in family holidays. Once again, this is an example of a continuing relationship being fostered between earthly parent and spirit child.

I would like to point out that both Kimberly and Nicole are well-adjusted women who are not prone to flights of fancy. They believe that their girls are part of the family and the girls have accepted their offers to stay as members of the family.

My experiences with abortion, however, are different. It is

rare for me to have lengthy conversations with aborted babies. As mentioned before, other spirits often speak for them. This may be due to the fact that their mothers chose not to create a relationship with them on earth and may not even consider that such a connection could be possible. Another reason why I don't have conversations could be that my work includes identifiers, which help the sitter to know with whom I'm speaking. These identifiers, such as gender, name, personality, illness, and physical descriptions, are not available to me or to the mother in cases of abortion.

However, this doesn't mean that the spirits of these babies go away. They don't. As mentioned, the spirit lights that I see over a woman's shoulder years after an abortion takes place are visual reminders of that fact.

Do the spirits of miscarried or aborted babies try to find other parents on earth so they can have another chance at life?

Spirits are alive and they always stress that point. Therefore, being born doesn't give them life but it does provide them with an opportunity to learn by experiencing life within the limits of a physical body. One of these learning experiences includes death. The spirits don't judge the value of a life by its length, but rather by how much they learned about how to give and receive love.

When a woman named Jane came to see me years ago, I was surprised that her mother in spirit admitted she had considered aborting Jane. She explained that she had been a teenager at the time and wasn't ready to have a child. In the end, Jane's mother decided to have the baby anyway and raised Jane with the help of her own family. An outsider looking at Jane's life would see that she had a loving and giving family surrounding her. What Jane didn't understand was why she had struggled all her life with deep feelings of being unwanted, of being unloved. In some way, her spirit was born into the physical body, still imprinted with feelings that may have been the result of her mother's deep ambivalence during the time of the pregnancy. Through her reunion with her mother in spirit, Jane gained understanding of and freedom from her confused feelings. As a result, her love for her mother grew even more.

Spirits aren't desperate to grab just any life or any available body. From what the spirits have told me, becoming incarnated isn't a random event. An incarnation is very important, and so spirits are willing to wait for the right situation to come along. Among their considerations are the attributes of an entire family line, the personalities of the parents, the combination of the parents' DNA, and the birth order.

During a particularly memorable (and unusual) session with a woman who works as a teacher of metaphysics, I was stunned to see a number of spirit babies with her. There was one speaker for all of them. The speaker made it clear that the babies were to be born to women in a group this very instructor was teaching at the time. Some of these women, the speaker said, had been unable to have children previously. This information was confirmed by the metaphysical teacher sitting with me. Several women in her group had recently become pregnant against the odds. It was very clear to me that these spirits were choosing to be born at this time in history to these particular women. There was the distinct feeling that their births were ordained.

Although this phenomenon begs many questions and engenders much speculation, the spirits, in this case, didn't provide an in-depth explanation. But in speaking with their representative, I was given the knowledge (almost by osmosis, it seems) that this group of women had been driven to embrace a spiritual approach to life, partly by the disappointment, grief, and struggles around getting pregnant. Their bonding as they explored matters of the spirit created the perfect invitation to a group of wise and determined souls.

I wouldn't be the first to recognize that many children born in the last twenty years are sometimes disturbingly mature for their ages and wise far beyond their years. As the consciousness of our country and the world continues to progress and acceptance of the spiritual in everyday life grows, those who choose to be born now are bringing needed gifts to move the evolution of our species forward.

In telling this story, I'm reminded that all the babies I've met in spirit, even those not born yet, are less concerned about what their soul needs than with how they will serve others in love. Their purpose is not limited by the number of minutes or years they have or have not spent on earth.

Frankly, compared with eternity, *all* of our lives on earth are short. I point this out because I've never heard from a baby who has left this earth before walking that they wanted a longer incarnation. The sense I receive from spirit babies is very much, "I got what I needed," or, "I've accomplished what was necessary."

When a spirit is considering an incarnation, they're aware that it may end with abortion or miscarriage. Being born and growing up in a body may not be the spirit's sole purpose. What is experienced from inception to death, the long or the short of it, is nothing less than what is required by the spirit, the mother, and the family.

Is it possible that my child now is one of my previously miscarried children?

I hesitate to say that anything is impossible, usually because once I do, I learn otherwise! In answer to this question, what I would say is this: yes, it is possible that if you had a miscarriage, the spirit of that miscarried baby could decide to incarnate at a later date. However, it is important to keep in mind that the spirit may have received what it needed during the first go-round. Also, I've spoken with spirits of those who passed by miscarriage and although they remain with the family in spirit, their mothers have borne children subsequent to the miscarriage.

Is it possible for miscarried or aborted children to be born into the same extended family as the mother who originally conceived them?

In theory, it is possible. In practice, however, I haven't actually had a spirit tell me of such plans. Of course, it is easy to understand why they wouldn't. Life is complicated enough without a woman who has lost a child thinking that her sister has given birth to the one she lost. This would be a bit like spiritual surrogacy. Please keep in mind that if a spirit is looking for a specific incarnation, any alteration in the parents changes the conditions and circumstances of the incarnation. For the most part, it doesn't seem to me as though spirits bounce from one mother to another in a family with the attitude of, "If it doesn't work with you, I'll have to make it happen with somebody else."

Do ancestors reincarnate within the family line?

I wish that the spirits discussed reincarnation with me a bit more. For the most part, though, the spirits I speak with want to discuss their most recent lives with their loved ones here on earth. The past can be effectively dealt with in the present incarnation because any unfinished healing and learning are brought along with us into our current lives.

One of the reasons that those in spirit are so interested in bringing healing to the current generation is because their own future incarnations may be affected by it. When I speak with ancestors from centuries ago, they will point out repetitive behaviors, some of which haven't changed in many generations. For instance, a long-dead seafaring captain told a young man well down the family line that he'd always feel the need to have a boat. The young man confirmed that not only was this true, but that all the men in his family had boats or worked in shipping. The old salt explained to the young man that he would need to help his young wife overcome the fear that he would be lost at sea. It turns out that the captain had died at sea, leaving a young widow behind. The young man confirmed this as a well-known family story that had worried many along the family line, including his own bride. The echoes of the past are often heard in the present. However, it is only in the present generation that the echoes can be silenced.

There are instances in which a spirit will mention that he and the sitter have been together for more than one lifetime. During a session in Laguna, California, a father in spirit mentioned a number of past lives he had shared with his son. Their relationship had not been the same in every lifetime, he told me. The father went on to describe a past life in which he and his son were clockmakers in a town in Germany, which he showed me on a map. The son looked at me with complete shock because he had just returned from a trip to that same area of Germany where he was drawn to the clock shops and even bought a watch. Although he and his father had been clock-makers in Germany in an earlier century, in this life they were Americans of German descent. There was a feeling that they had remained in the family line, but I didn't receive details that would have allowed for that to be researched.

If someone aborts a baby who, in a past life, may have been an ancestor, does it destroy the destiny of that person's family?

I've learned from the spirits that every action we take has an effect on earth and in heaven. Nothing is without conse-quence, and we don't live or die in a vacuum. From the broader perspective of the spirits, however, what looks like destruction to us is always an opportunity for change leading to transforma-tion. So yes, aborting a child who may have been an ancestor can shift or change the family's destiny, but from the spirits' perspective, nothing is destroyed.

Spirit SUMMARY

When a pregnancy is ended by abortion or miscarriage, a mother may experience feelings of guilt, disappointment, and grief. If a baby is born and then later passes, sometimes for no discernible reason, the sense of loss may be complicated by feel-ings of failure, blame, and anger. But the spirits of these babies remain with their families, offering guidance, joy, and healing.

9

It's Just Wrong

Murder, Genocide, and Other Crimes Against Humanity

Spirit TWEET

"Dying doesn't make you nice." (Said by a young man in spirit when asked if he met his murderer.)

Spirit THOUGHTS

A Case of Mistaken Identity

The little girl in spirit standing before me was staring straight at me with large, round, very dark eyes. Her face was framed by black curly hair that fell to her shoulders. *This is Anne Frank*, I thought.

As a preteen, I had read *The Diary of a Young Girl* surreptitiously at night by flashlight hidden in a tent of sheets and blankets. Anne Frank's story affected me deeply, the unwritten ending of her life even more so. When I saw this little girl in spirit I thought my chance had finally come for direct communication with someone whose life experience I greatly valued.

The young girl before me, however, looked much younger

than Anne Frank would have been at the time she was hiding behind walls and writing in her diary. That wasn't enough to dissuade me from believing it was her, however, because spirits can appear as younger or older versions of themselves.

This must *be Anne Frank*, I thought. "No, I'm not!" was the responding thought from the little girl.

It was then that I noticed all the spirits standing around her. They looked to be at a train station. Dressed in their best, they had luggage in their hands and were lined up behind the woman who had come to see me. I caught a few names as they tossed them into my thoughts. I assumed, of course, that these were the people the lady had come to see.

Not so.

As I relayed more detailed information provided by the spirits to her, including that they had died in concentration camps during World War II, the woman was even less willing to acknowledge their presence.

I didn't understand. Members of her family had died under inhumane circumstances, yet she didn't want to talk with them. I was dismayed, to say the very least.

But this sitter hadn't set an appointment to speak with relatives who died in the Holocaust even though they wanted to speak with her. She was there to connect with a friend who had died recently and to see if her beloved cat was still with her.

During our session together, I conversed with her friend, and the cat made a brief appearance, too. The tableau of the sitter's relatives all standing in line quietly behind her, waiting patiently, was visible to me the whole time. Just as we were ending the session, the little spirit girl with the big dark eyes looked at me . . . and smiled.

This little girl's smile stayed with me for quite some time thereafter. She and the others I saw that day had died during one of the great horrors of the twentieth century. Despite this fact, she appeared wearing her best dress, even though it may have been the last dress she ever wore. While she may have experienced a terrifying end to her short life on earth, she was smiling. That touched me in a deeper way than I can describe. I couldn't get past thinking about *how* she died; she wouldn't let me forget the fact that, despite the intentions of her captors, she was *alive*.

Unlike Anne Frank, this little girl already knew the end of her story on earth by the time I had met her. Yet she *still* smiled at me. That smile seemed as mysterious at the time as the Mona Lisa's.

The little spirit girl I met years ago is the one who inspired this chapter. I think about her whenever I see a story on the news about murder and brutality anywhere in the world.

Spirits Answer a 911 Call

"Turn on the TV—we're at war!" said the voice on the phone, waking me from a sound sleep early on September 11, 2001.

Both the caller and I are New Yorkers by birth; she had lived in the city, and I had lived in the suburbs. We both had relatives and friends still living and working in Manhattan. As we shared stories with friends and coworkers in the days following that dreadful day, it was astounding how many people we knew who were directly affected when the planes crashed and the towers fell.

Death, even on the largest scale, remains personal. Each individual who dies is a mother or father, sister or brother, son or daughter. In the work that I do, the pain caused by sudden and seemingly senseless death is healed one person at a time. I have to believe this and bear it in mind or I could easily become overwhelmed by the grief of those left behind.

Throughout my younger years, traumatic energy at a location would completely engulf me. In fact, when I was ten years old, I was carried from a Gettysburg battlefield because I couldn't stop crying. What started as a history lesson resulted in the knowledge that there were some historical sites I couldn't manage very well. Even with that understanding, I have still been overwhelmed when visiting countries where there has been tremendous bloodshed. In Cambodia, for instance, I could barely touch my feet to the ground without some sense of the terror and mass murder that took place there. Fortunately, by the time I visited that country, I had learned how to manage these feelings, for the most part. However, I'm less able to shield myself from the response of the spirits and the grief of their loved ones when I have personal family ties to the area, as I do to New York.

That's why on September 12, I said to those who had died the day before, "Don't come at me all at once." I *wanted* to help people whose lives had changed. I *knew* that I could help, but I needed to do so for each in turn.

As so often happens in my dealings with spirits, they had other plans. Friends of mine pressured me into getting together a week after the day of the attack. "We'll form a circle and pray for the families," my friend Andrea suggested. *This sounds positive and well contained,* I thought.

Put a medium in a room with loving, well-intentioned people who are also sensitive to the spirits, and more than prayer is bound to happen. Within minutes, my living room was filled with spirits giving us their names and telling us that they weren't missing. They had seen their photos and frantic notes from loved ones plastered everywhere. They had heard friends and family asking anyone they could about their whereabouts. These spirits knew their loved ones still held the hope that they were lost rather than dead. From the spirits' perspective, it was important to convey that they were not lost at all. It was important to assure others that they were okay.

One lady in spirit very purposely walked up to Andrea and gave her full name, explaining that she had been working under her married name so her maiden name's appearance on the list of those missing was incorrect. She wanted her loved ones to know.

In the middle of all this intensity, with spirits eager to communicate, I was relieved to see the helper spirits show up. They appeared almost as efficient Red Cross or government aid workers. Equipped with clipboards and pens, they started checking people's names off their lists. Each person in spirit was then guided to a place beyond a purple door that had appeared in my living room. One by one, they disappeared from sight until the room was empty and silent and peaceful.

I was impressed with how well organized the effort was from the spirits' side of things. No matter how chaotic the scene was on September 11, I have no doubt that each person who passed on that day was personally attended to by either someone they knew in spirit or a helper who guided them on their way.

I have talked before about how everyone is escorted personally into the afterlife, but it was amazing to see the attention given to the spirits of this event. Just as we have first responders here on earth, the other side has first responders as well. Spirit "greeters" lend help in ways similar to the way in which volunteers help people on earth.

For instance, right before Thanksgiving, a mother in spirit who had passed sometime prior to September 11 told her daughter through me that she was inviting all the new arrivals in the afterlife to a Thanksgiving dinner there. "That makes perfect sense to me," her daughter replied. "Mom always invited people who were new to the neighborhood to our house for Thanksgiving. Of course she would do the same thing in the afterlife."

After any major traumatic event, whether man-made or brought about by nature, there is often an outpouring of assistance and resources to help ease the suffering of those left behind. Individual citizens donate money, from pennies to millions of dollars. Fund-raising concerts and telethons encourage people worldwide to pool their funds to provide the aid that is needed. At times like these, the inherent understanding that "what happens to one of us, happens to all of us" is expressed in a mighty way. This is actually the way that the spirits see things *all* of the time, not just in times of crisis. Where we see separation, they see connection. When buildings and lives on earth literally crumble, imagined divisions between us spiritually crumble too.

Although earthquakes, tsunamis, the methodical killing of a targeted race, and the felling of towers by planes on a course of destruction and death have occurred on a mass scale, these events are all personal. The spirits won't let us forget that.

When disaster strikes somewhere in the world, the news stories that follow invariably include interviews with people who talk about how they simply felt "moved" or "compelled" to help strangers, even if they are from other nations and cultures. Often, they will say about their gestures of support, "I don't know why I felt that I needed to do this, but I did." When people halfway around the world are driven to make a difference in a stranger's life, it is because no matter how big the need, the call is still personal. The spirits make it that way. They move us to help their loved ones, one person at a time.

Growing up in America, I've always been struck by how independent we think we are. In my work with the spirits, they keep showing and telling me how *interdependent* we are.

Years after September 11, 2001, and far from New York City, the spirits reminded me again that I could help, one person at a time.

THE ROSE STILL BLOOMS
Just remember in the winter far beneath the bitter snows
Lies the seed that with the sun's love
In the spring becomes the rose.

The final note of the song fell to silence. No one in the audience took a breath. For some reason, I had been inspired to end an evening of spirit communication by leading the group in an a capella version of the song. What I didn't know was that this song had special meaning for a family in the audience. It was the favorite song of a young woman who had died when the towers of the World Trade Center collapsed. A few days later, I met this beautiful and charming spirit when her parents came to me for a session.

"Everybody loves this girl!" I exclaimed. "I can see why. She's got a bubbly personality and loves life. She's irrepressible.

She wanted to live in New York City, but in her heart, she's a small town girl."

The parents sitting with me were grief-stricken, and I understood why when in my mind, I saw a film of the World Trade Center collapsing. Earlier in our conversation, this delightful young woman had shown me a honeybee hive that was the symbol for the ancient word from which her name was derived. She had shared details of her life, which only her parents would know and understand. She talked about things that had happened since her death so that they would be reassured that she was still present in their lives.

All in all, she communicated very well with a medium.

"Your daughter was always running late," she's telling me. "So at first, you thought that she had avoided the destruction."

"Yes, that's right," her father said. The love for his daughter and his pride in her accomplishments was evident in every word he spoke and every gesture he made. He was also very solicitous of his wife, who could not be consoled.

"She's telling me that she wanted to help. She was killed as the pieces came down. She died helping people. You know that's the kind of person she is."

I loved talking with this enthusiastic young woman. She charged up the room with her energy so that the hair on my arms and my head stood up on end. It was like sitting in the midst of a room filled with static electricity.

Although she had died during an event that catapulted us all into a different world, she took her part in it in stride; she died doing what she always did, helping others. What she really wanted was to let her family know that she wasn't scared when she died, that she survived death, and that she loved them.

There were no grand speeches. There were no political statements. Intent to destroy had not destroyed her . . . or her loving spirit.

It Isn't How It Looks

For those of us who lived in the United States before 2001, acts of terror were not the norm. However, in other countries around the world, this is not the case and hasn't been for years. In some cities, enjoying coffee at a street café can be a death-defying act. I was reminded of that fact when a woman named Lillian came to see me.

"There's a man in spirit standing next to you. He gives me the feeling of husband and a name that sounds like 'Sol,' like the sun. Your husband is a powerful man. He's talking to me about movies. He speaks like a producer."

"Oh yes, that was his career," she said.

"He comes with a young woman. She gives me the feeling that she is your daughter."

Lillian, the woman sitting in front of me had the grace, the beauty and presence of a former actress. She was extremely well composed for someone who had lost both her husband and daughter.

Lillian's husband created a movie in my head, a miniature cinematic masterpiece showing father and daughter sitting at a café table, chatting. It was a peaceful, sunny day until—BOOM! With blinding white light, the movie ended.

Neither Sol nor his daughter remained fixated on the movie that they had shown. They were more interested in talking about family matters, a new baby that was about to be born into the family, a little boy. They talked about the daughter's schooling and her interest in pursuing a writing career. Lillian's daughter mentioned that she was with her mother while she was reading through the stories she had written as a child. Sol attempted to sing a few Dean Martin songs, badly.

I've spoken with many spirits who have died violent deaths. Except in rare cases, the young do not focus on the violence. Instead, they talk about the details of life rather than the details of death. Many have told me that they were spared any pain in passing. One young woman in spirit told her parents, "I watched it happen. Nothing hurt me."

I spoke with a young man in spirit who had been tortured, murdered, and his body burned beyond recognition. When he spoke with his father, he described his room in their family home, including details such as his sports car calendar, and his loving relationship with his father and the rest of the family. This young man did not reinforce his father's nightmares by dwelling on how he had died. He was not reliving the horrific circumstances of his death in the afterlife, nor did he want his father to relive them here on earth.

Time and again I've been told by kids that the way they died is not the way they live in eternity. It is a memory that they can choose not to visit.

One young girl who had been cut with a machete and subsequently bled to death likened the experience to being born. "When I was born, it was a bloody mess. Being born into the afterlife was messy too," she said. I learned later that her mother had bled profusely at her birth.

The worst trauma that we can imagine seems to have the least effect on those who have died as a result of it. In the afterlife, kids do not continue living in the midst of horror. And they do their best to keep their parents from residing in that horror here on earth.

Mind What You Say

As a medium, I'm always listening to what spirits have to say. Messages may consist of words, symbols, images, and sensations. Over the years, I've gotten good at translating what can be obtuse "spirit speak" into understandable "people speak." As a medium, I've also learned to listen to the silences, because sometimes what isn't voiced is as illuminating as what is actually said.

This is particularly true in murders or cataclysmic events. Whether death was caused by human hands or by forces of nature, one surprising consistency stands out.

Spirits do not refer to themselves as "victims."

We, on the other hand, are quick to label *everyone* a victim. Turn on the evening news and you can hear phrases like "victims of a hurricane" or "the victims of a convicted serial killer."

One young man in spirit brought me up short when I referred to him as a victim.

He had been shot and killed while driving in his car by someone targeting highway drivers. As I was speaking with him and passing along messages to his mother, it suddenly occurred to me that I had seen a news story about his death. *Oh, I know who you are,* I said to him in my mind. *Your story was on the news. You're a victim of the . . .*

Before I could finish the thought, he cut me off with, "I'm not a victim." And that was that.

"Your son doesn't see himself as a victim," I told his mother.

"I didn't raise my son to be a victim of anyone or anything," she responded proudly.

Spirits are not physically vulnerable as they were on earth; they don't wear badges in heaven that say "victim."

Those in spirit also don't speak in "what ifs." They don't postulate about what could have happened or what should have happened or not. They present what "is" with an astonishing amount of calm and peace. This can be a bit unnerving, especially when family members are looking for someone to blame, or for information that would confirm their own sense of justice.

A woman who suspected that her brother-in-law had poisoned her sister demanded, "Ask my sister to tell you if her husband killed her. I might be the only one in the family who thinks so, but I *know* I'm right." The sister in spirit refused to point the finger.

When one mother wasn't satisfied with the verdict received as the result of a jury trial, she asked her son in spirit if she should sue in civil court. The son, who had been in law enforcement, said, "I'm okay. I know that you love me."

"I do love you with all my heart," she said, crying.

"I don't need a verdict where I'm living now. If you go to court, do it because you need to for yourself, not for me," he said, releasing her from her self-imposed obligation to defend him beyond death.

I learned later that in her quest, she had become estranged from her second son and nearly destroyed her marriage.

The arm of the law is long, but it doesn't reach the afterlife. It doesn't need to.

The idea that someone who is murdered won't rest until the murder is solved might make good Hollywood-style entertainment. A mystery novel where the bad guys get caught might be a satisfying read. But in my world, murder isn't entertaining and justice doesn't always bring healing.

The Balancing Act

A man in his early twenties, who had been gunned down near a convenience store, taught me the difference between justice on earth . . . and love from heaven.

His nickname was Rally, because he loved racing cars. When he came to visit his mother and aunt at a small event, he took right over.

"I'm seeing lots of cars with fancy paint jobs," I told his mother.

"He loved to work on cars on the weekend," his mother, Tisha, replied. She was a beautiful, petite woman with almond-shaped eyes who didn't look much older than a teenager herself.

"You're wearing him around your neck, he's telling me. He likes his face in gold."

From underneath her blouse, she took out a square gold pendant. The face of a young man was etched on its surface. It was barely visible.

"Rally is showing me lots of flowers and candles on the sidewalk. I see stuffed animals, even balloons and lots of people standing along the block."

"Yeah, lots of people come to the spot where he died."

"He's showing me jail bars and giving me the feeling that one person is already in jail because of what happened."

"Yes, that's right," she replied.

"But he's in jail because of something else, not because your son is dead, right?"

"Nothing was proved around my son's death. It's just not right," she said, suddenly looking years older.

"He didn't die right away, he's telling me, but he didn't feel the pain. He wants you to know that." Rally said "brother" in my ear and showed me a flash photo of a young man standing over him. "Your younger son found him, right?" I asked his mother.

She nodded yes.

Rally described the car with the gunman inside. Although witnesses had seen the car, no one came forward with information regarding the shooter. Rally showed me himself spinning at the sound of the first shot and covering the girl walking next to him.

"He protected her," Rally's mother said. "It's just not right that my baby died. It's just not right."

"Rally is showing me a playground. It has swings, one of those spinning things and a broken seesaw, a teeter-totter," I continued. "He stood up to the bullies at the playground, he's telling me."

"Yeah, he was a fighter, my Rally. There's a park right by our house. I used to take him there. I don't remember seein' no teeter-totter, though."

In my mind, I asked Rally, *What's with the teeter-totter?*

It was then that he showed me a picture in my mind of the scales of justice. That didn't seem to make any more sense, but I shared that with his mother.

"Yeah, justice," she said. "No justice for my son. It don't matter if that statue be on the courthouse."

I knew that Rally was trying to make a point and that I (and his mother) didn't completely understand. Fortunately, spirits can be patient.

Rally flashed the picture of the teeter-totter into my mind again. This time, the word "LOVE" in big letters sat right in the middle of it, and it was perfectly straight, perfectly balanced.

When I gave this image to Rally's mother, she said, "Yeah, that's my baby. He's always talkin' 'bout love."

These words stayed with me: "always talkin' 'bout love." This young man did more than just talk about love, though. He put love into action. His last act on earth was to shield someone else from a barrage of bullets.

I thought about Rally, the teeter-totter of love, and the scales of justice. Those images remained in my mind for a long, long time.

Over the years, I've used Rally's teeter-totter as a metaphor for the heavenly standard by which we all judge ourselves in the afterlife. Does what was given balance that which was taken? Does love expressed balance love withheld? Did we love others more than ourselves? Or were our needs more important than anyone else's? When we sit down on one side of the teeter-totter opposite our actions on the other seat, will it remain in balance?

In my work with the spirits, I present their cases for perfect and balanced love here on earth because that is the energy they bring to me. It is the force of their energetic love that can inspire change here on earth.

Sending You Love

When I talk to kids in spirit who have been murdered, they often skip right over the details of their passing because they're more interested in comforting and inspiring their parents, and the public at large, to bring about change.

Oddly enough, one of the first ways they do this is to talk about their funerals.

This might seem a bit morbid, but the kids see it as anything but. Kids don't come to their own funerals in a Tom Sawyer kind of way—to see what people are saying about them—they're there to be part of the love and support for their parents and families.

One young man told me that he loved a good party. His parents agreed that his friends took over the event and with live music and video made it a night to remember.

Kids in spirit get a kick out of telling me that there isn't enough room in the church, the hall, or the auditorium to hold all the people who want to attend the memorial or funeral. This is in no way a form of self-aggrandizement; it is their way of reminding their parents that their lives here mattered and that they will not be forgotten.

Kids use the arms of other people to touch and hug their parents. Every e-mail, card, casserole dinner, shared photo, and Facebook post are ways that kids in spirit inspire people to surround their parents with love. Depending on how well publicized their death is, a kid in spirit can inspire hundreds, if not thousands, on earth to express love and support for their grieving parents. This support may in turn inspire the parents to spearhead new initiatives to protect the children of others through legislation or law enforcement. As tragic as it may seem to us, a murder—even under the worst of circumstances—can be used by spirits to raise awareness of how we can take better care of each other.

A Wedding Gift

The love of those in spirit can bring about healing despite the grisliest of circumstances underlying their deaths.

One night during a development circle, a young spirit appeared and started talking about how she died. She made it clear that she was "related" to one of the women in our circle, not by blood but by pending marriage. She had been killed two weeks before her own wedding took place.

Kathy, a beautiful woman in her early twenties, was wrapping up things at work late one night and was murdered right at her desk. She provided me with specific details, far too graphic to mention here out of respect for the family. Despite how horrific these details were, this young woman didn't once call herself a victim, didn't place blame and didn't tell me to catch her killer. She had something else in mind altogether.

I had to wait seven years to find out what it was.

"My sister told me a while ago that you had spoken to my fiancée," the man on the phone said. "I'll be flying into Los Angeles and would like to make an appointment."

Immediately, I knew who he was. This, I must admit is unusual, especially as years had passed since I met his fiancée in spirit. This was much more than just "a while ago." Details of this young woman's murder, however, remained written in my memory as though in indelible ink.

When her fiancé walked in, I was struck by his posture. Charles was a pilot in the navy and that was evident with every step he took. He sat upright in his chair, an expectant look on his face. I knew who he wanted to speak with, but of course, I couldn't guarantee that she, or anyone else, would come forward.

And then, there she was . . . in a red dress.

"Kathy is standing right next to you in a red dress. She says that the only photo you have of her is in that red dress."

"That's true," he said as he pulled a photo out of his brief-case. "She didn't like having her photo taken."

The rest of our time together was spent with Kathy mentioning members of her family, a recent ceremony in which Charles received a commendation, and the new house he had just bought. There wasn't one mention of her manner of death, no details, no blood. The only red in the room was her dress.

"It is okay for you to get married," Kathy said, out of the blue. "I love you and I want you to be happy."

The navy pilot's eyes filled with tears. As a tear slid down his cheek unchecked, he said, "That's why I'm here today. I needed to hear that Kathy was okay with my plans before I could go forward with them. I stopped in Los Angeles on my way to meet my new bride."

Then it was time for tears to fill my eyes.

The communication that started with wedding bells stilled by murder seven years before had ended with wedding bells ringing again. Whether Kathy's murderer was brought to justice, I don't know. What I do know is that Kathy wanted love for the man she loved, more than justice for the man who killed her.

Spirit ANSWERS

Do all bad people go to hell? Or do some end up in heaven?

First of all, people in the afterlife have different ideas about what constitutes a "bad" person. A woman in spirit who had been very religious on earth seemed surprised when she saw her non-believing brother again after she passed. "They let anybody into heaven!" she exclaimed. Apparently, her brother was the black sheep of the family, but a beloved one all the same. A young man in spirit summed up the hell/heaven difference succinctly. He told his mother, "Dying doesn't make you nice. I like staying with nice people." I agree with this young man. I like staying with the nice people too, especially when I work with spirits.

I get asked all the time what hell is like. Since I haven't been there myself, I can't give firsthand knowledge. However, the spirits have told me many times that our actions on earth create our reality in the afterlife. For those who have with intent hurt their fellow creatures, their reality in the afterlife is populated by those with similar intentions. It is hard to imagine what it would be like having all murderers living together. If there isn't a sign over that place that says, "Welcome to hell," I'd be surprised.

Is my loved one in heaven unable to rest peacefully until justice is served for her death?

The spirits often speak with me about experiencing peace in heaven that we can't understand here on earth. Along with this exceptional peace is a sense of being safe. Kids on the other side are surrounded by the love of their families. I haven't spoken with a spirit yet for whom justice on earth is a prerequisite for peace in heaven. Fortunately, loved ones in spirit no longer have to carry the pain of what the body has suffered. This doesn't mean, however, that those who break the law and cause suffering should not be brought to justice. What it does mean is that even though there may not be sufficient evidence to convict or the punishment doesn't seem equal to the crime, we have not failed our loved one in spirit. Justice on earth has limitations. The good news is that loved ones in spirit live in peace and love beyond those limitations.

What if the police never find the person who killed them?

No one can evade being caught forever. No one's actions can remain hidden in the afterlife and no one escapes judgment for those actions. *No one.* It is the same way with all of us. Justifications and rationalities fall away and actions stand darkly in contrast to the bright light of perfect love.

If someone is murdered, does his spirit have a chance to confront his killer when he dies?

I haven't had a spirit tell me that he is waiting to greet his killer. What I have been shown in visions and dreams is that those who cause a separation between people who love each other experience the full effect of being cut off from love. There is no need to confront a killer because he is finally immersed in the realization of how his actions have affected others. If the pool of compassion in a person's heart is shallow on earth, the ocean of remorse he drowns in is much deeper when he reaches the afterlife.

When someone dies in a big event that makes the news, why does that spirit talk about everyday things rather than the event that caused his or her death?

Sometimes when I'm communicating with the spirits, even silly details take on greater significance. For instance, one mother in spirit told her daughter that she was with her in the store that day—and she even named the brand of toilet paper her daughter picked out. Although that seems like a ridiculous thing to talk about, this toilet paper had special meaning for her daughter. Those we love share in the details of our lives, even the most intimate of details like what toilet paper is our favorite kind. The spirits mention these details of everyday life because they are reminders of love. Spirits prefer reminding us of the love shared rather than the pain experienced because of their death.

Spirit SUMMARY

People who die as the result of horrific crime do not have to relive the circumstances of their passing until the perpetrators of the crime against them are brought to justice. Spirits don't see themselves as victims, but rather as agents of change here on earth. In situations when many people die at one time, each person is taken care of personally by other spirits sent to guide them through their dying experience. The outpouring of love for families left behind following an epic disaster is inspired by the love that those in spirit are sending them from heaven.

Bringing Heaven Home

How Kids Say "Hi" from the Other Side

𝒮𝓅𝒾𝓇𝒾𝓉 TWEET

"I went to the funeral before I died." (Said by a young man whose memorial was on the day before he was removed from life support.)

𝒮𝓅𝒾𝓇𝒾𝓉 THOUGHTS

Keeping Up Appearances

"Your son is telling me that you saw him with your own eyes after he died," I said to the mother sitting across from me. "He was standing in the doorway to your bedroom."

"I *knew* it wasn't a dream," she said. "My son really *was* standing there." She seemed relieved that her experience was being confirmed by her son through me. Apparently, no one else, including her husband, believed that such a thing was possible.

Seeing spirits is not only possible but becoming more probable each day. The reason that this is so isn't because the spirits have changed their tactics; it is because *we* have changed our mind-sets. With the ever-increasing acceptance of spirit communication, it is easier for those living in the spirit world to make their presence known in ours.

When I first started presenting public evenings of spirit communication, I would ask how many people had seen a medium in person. More often than not, only a few hands were raised. These days, the opposite is true.

That's not to say that there won't be people reading this book that have never seen a medium or experienced a spirit connection. That's okay too. The spirits will meet you wherever you are and walk forward with you from that point.

Over the years, I've noticed that more people are reporting direct communication from their loved ones in spirit *after* meeting with a medium or attending an event. Sometimes just being in the room with spirit energy can jump-start awareness. During private sessions, I can feel the spirits practicing on me as though they're learning the best way to get their points across. If I were a little less confident in serving the spirits, I might think that they are rendering the work of mediums obsolete. Instead, what I really think is happening is that the spirits are teaching us *all* that communication is an inclusive activity, not an exclusive one for the privileged few.

Like everything else in our world, mediumship is changing. It seems to me that the role of the medium is shifting from being the only person to connect you to your loved ones into being the person who can actually help you increase your own awareness and connections. It has been rewarding to see mediumship evolve into something more of a collective effort and experience over the years. The spirits seem to be pushing us all to work together to create a new way of relating to those living in the spirit world and on earth. At events, via e-mail and on Facebook, people are asking me to explain or interpret what their loved ones are trying to say to them rather than asking me *if* their loved ones are around.

This is particularly true when it pertains to kids in spirit. We really shouldn't be surprised by this. After all, we're the ones who taught them to call when they reached their destination. Why should getting to heaven be any different? Kids want us to know that they've arrived and that they're safe. Many kids aren't satisfied with a simple flicker of the lights to let their parents know that they're around. Their appearances can be energetic and dramatic, hip and amusing, or downright silly, just like kids themselves.

Two days before I started to write this chapter, I had a session that reminded me of where spirit communication is headed.

A New Walk of Life

A very self-possessed lady named Dawn came to see me. She was dressed in black and red, with a string of pearls at her neck and her hair pulled back severely into a bun.

As Dawn sat down, I could feel a group gathering around us. At first I felt a bit overwhelmed and asked everyone to settle down. Out of the corner of my eye, I saw a cream-and-peach striped male cat in spirit sitting on the floor next to us. Dawn acknowledged that she had a cat just like that years ago. She loved that cat. The cat flashed a couple of fast pictures in my mind—of two dogs! The first was a dark-colored mutt with lots of terrier in him and the second, a purebred little princess that looked like a Shih Tzu. Dawn confirmed that she had recently gotten two dogs of that description. The cat impressed upon me that the little princess dog would just sit down when she was done walking and would demand to be carried. That was accurate, Dawn said. I thought to myself, *It's just like a cat to have so much to say about dogs.* But then the cat gave me the feeling that since the princess dog wouldn't go for long walks, Dawn needed some encouragement to go walking. Dawn agreed that she had been planning to start a walking regimen with or without the dogs. The cat impressed upon me that the walking wouldn't be just for exercise, but would give Dawn the opportunity to pursue a creative project, a book with the word "walk" in the title. Dawn gasped.

"Yes," she said. "I'm thinking about a book, and the word 'walk' is in the title." I could tell that she was about to give me the title. I asked her not to tell me anything about it, because other spirits might want to discuss this project as well. Charlie, the cat, showed me a picture in my mind of him walking with Dawn around a lake or a reservoir. "That's where I was planning on walking," said Dawn. The cat would be walking with her.

As I glanced away from the cat, I saw a female in spirit standing next to Dawn, who gave me a sister connection, and I heard the words "breast cancer" in my head. Dawn's sister had died from breast cancer. Her sister told me that she was with a man, a father figure, who was in the process of dying with cancer. Dawn confirmed that her stepfather was dying of cancer and the family was setting things up for hospice care. Dawn's sister, Virginia, said that she was with the stepfather, whom she loved dearly, and he was starting to see her. Virginia wanted Dawn to know that if her father (spirits often drop "step," "half," etc.) mentioned that she was visiting him, Dawn should know that he really was seeing her and not imagining it.

I also heard the word "suicide" in my ear, said close enough to suggest that someone was standing next to me, leaning in, and whispering a secret to me. Then I could see a man drawing in close to Dawn. He said, "Martin," "work," and "Texas" in short succession. I told Dawn that a man in spirit associated with work was giving me the name Martin and the state, Texas. Dawn's eyes flew open wide. "Martin was a coworker of mine. He killed himself. While on a business trip to Texas a week ago, I was talking about him with others in his office." I could hear the laughter of those in spirit who surrounded us that seemed an odd contrast to the idea of suicide.

"Wow," I said. "Martin was a real jokester, very upbeat, and lots of fun. It must have been a shock when he died, because he seemed so upbeat all the time, right?" Dawn agreed that it had been a shock. Martin always had a joke at the ready and a kind word. He went on to name and describe in detail the person who replaced him and told Dawn that he would work on her behalf to streamline the transition. Martin told Dawn to continue to consult him about work-related issues. When something "off the wall" at work made her laugh, she would know that Martin was around.

Aunt Gloria was the next person to make an appearance. Aunt Gloria was a no-nonsense battle-ax (*her* description of herself, not mine). Dawn agreed. Aunt Gloria said that Dawn needed help in dealing with her mother. Aunt Gloria said that Dawn's mother was in complete denial about her husband's illness and was making no preparations for his passing. In addition, Aunt Gloria said that Dawn's mother was fighting her every step of the way, from setting up doctor's appointments to arranging hospice care. She told Dawn that she would do her best to help ease her mother's fear because she had been through it herself. Aunt Gloria reminded Dawn that her own husband of fifty years had passed with cancer. She had taken care of him until the end. When Dawn smelled roses, she would know that Aunt Gloria was around.

Then I heard, "Mom!" A young man in spirit came up beside me and gave me the name "Chris." Chris, Dawn's son, went on not to describe his own passing, but to talk about the book that she would be writing. He said that he would walk the journey with her and inspire her along the way. (There's that word "walk" again.) He told his mother that he would help her to write about him. Dawn confirmed that she had decided to write a book about her experiences with her son.

And then Chris started joking. At least I hope he was joking when he said, "Mom, you don't need to spend money on a medium because I'm coming to you myself. You can see me!" I told Dawn that Chris wants to singlehandedly put me out of work. Dawn laughed and said that, weeks ago, she had felt Chris around her. When she turned to look, she saw him. Chris was thrilled that he was able to pull *that* one off. Dawn was glad that he mentioned it in our session. I told Dawn that more and more the spirits are asking me to validate people's own experiences with loved ones in spirit. It was then that Chris told me his mother had met with me more than a year prior. (I hadn't remembered.) After our meeting together, she increasingly felt Chris around her. As she became more open to his presence, he became bolder in his efforts to make contact.

"I'm so lucky," Dawn said. "Death is not the end of life. Relationships continue . . . in a different way. I really want to write a book that helps a lot people." Dawn spoke the words of my heart's desire as well.

I hesitated sharing Dawn's story for the simple reason that it might cause disappointment for other parents who desire to see their own children in spirit, and haven't. The greater acceptance of spirit communication has created higher expectations for hopeful sitters. As the "supernatural" became more natural in everyday life, I also began noticing that people were developing an anxiety different from any other that I'd seen before. People used to be anxious when they came to see me because they didn't understand how spirit communication worked. Nowadays people are anxious because although they're aware of their loved ones in spirit, they are afraid that they might somehow be missing their messages.

Friendly Greetings

"MY MOTHER CAME TO ME IN A DREAM. HER MOUTH WAS MOVING BUT SHE WASN'T SAYING ANYTHING," said an e-mail from a woman who was either frantic or left her caps lock on. "WHAT WAS SHE TRYING TO TELL ME?" she asked.

The ever increasing number of similar e-mails showing up in my inbox inspired me to create a workshop with a friend and associate of mine that would address not only the way that spirits say "hello," but the meaning and value of those communications. My friend Ken Newelt, a marriage and family therapist, came up with the title for the workshop, "Knock, Knock. Who's there?—Signs and Signals from the Other Side." This wasn't just a funny name for a workshop; spirits do actually knock sometimes to let us know that they're around.

For instance, when I was preparing for a session in Riverside, California, I heard a knock at the door. *Too early,* I thought.

When I opened the door no one was standing there. However, two people were sitting on a bench in the hallway. "Did you just knock?" I asked them. "No," they responded in unison. Then the words, "I thought you were Tom," popped out of my mouth. But when I double-checked my schedule, there was no appointment with a Tom listed. About fifteen minutes later there was another knock at the door. *Not again,* I thought. When I opened it, there stood the same two people who had been sitting in the hallway. They seemed a bit agitated and walked sideways into the room, keeping their eyes on me at all times. When we sat down to start, the young man said, "My mother and I came today to speak with my father, Tom. When you opened the door and said the name 'Tom,' we knew for sure that Dad was already here. He was *always* early. It was a little spooky, though."

When spirits knock on our door, it is only "spooky" if we allow it to be. One of the reasons why Ken and I presented the "Knock, Knock" workshop was to provide a safe environment so that people could leave their fears behind them when discussing the loving spirits who surround us.

During the workshop, we organized spirit communications into categories from the mundane to the complex. In mundane communications, the "hello" is usually something direct and very simple like the flickering of light or the wafting of a loved one's favorite perfume. More complex communications include instances in which the spirits inspire a third person to deliver their message, or cause physical items to disappear and/or reappear. Examples of complex communications will be discussed later on in this chapter.

Since I understand the spirits' language of energy, my experience helped workshop participants to understand what their loved ones were saying. Ken's knowledge with grief enabled people to process their feelings about this new way of relating to their loved ones.

One of the participants mentioned that while driving, she regularly smelled cigarette smoke. She explained that her father smoked and that she believed smoking had contributed to his death. She had always *hated* cigarettes, yet smelling smoke in her car now made her happy. So what was formerly a painful memory was now a comforting sign that her father was still with her. In a sense, the smell of his particular brand of cigarettes became his signature. A signature is nothing more than a consistent way that a spirit says, "I'm here."

Learning the Ropes

Not a week goes by that there aren't dozens of new examples of spirits letting their loved ones know that they're around. It would be wonderful if everyone experienced the full spirit body appearance as did the two mothers mentioned earlier in this chapter. However, I can't stress enough that an extraordinary appearance doesn't necessarily equate with the amount of love a spirit loved one is expressing. These boys don't love their mothers more than other sons in spirit love their mothers. There is a way I often suggest to think about it: just imagine if your little boy came home from kindergarten with a picture that he drew for you full of stick figures and squiggly lines. That picture would be proudly posted on the refrigerator, right? There would have been no expectation that your son was going to come home from kindergarten with a Rembrandt-like masterpiece.

It is the same way with the spirits. Some spirits are better than others at using energy to get their points across. Many spirits are like kindergarteners who are still learning the basics, while others are the Rembrandts of communication. That goes for us on the earth as well. Some people are innately attuned to the spirits and others need to work harder to master their spirit reception and communication skills.

I am interested in teaching people simple ways to set up communication with their loved ones in spirit. The first thing I tell people is: anticipate that communication will happen without expecting (or demanding) that it will occur in a certain prescribed way.

The story of one distraught mother drives this point home. She informed me that she had told her son in spirit to play a certain song at a particular time (the time at which he died) on three consecutive Wednesdays (the day on which he died). If he did that she would surely know he was with her. Unfortunately, this mother ended up being devastatingly disappointed when what she expected didn't occur. She had convinced herself that her son had abandoned her completely. Having worked with so many kids, I couldn't imagine that this was the truth. I thought it was much more likely that her son was in spirit communication kindergarten and that what she was asking him to do was too difficult a task for him to execute—it was the equivalent of asking him to create a Rembrandt.

The good news is that when she and I had a session together, her son mentioned several things that he had done to say "hello." His photo fell off the mantel and didn't break. He also turned the television on when his favorite football team was playing. Because his mother was so fixated on what she *expected* to him to do, she entirely missed what he was *able* to do. Anticipation without expectation is one of the prerequisites for a successful invitation to spirit communication. I'll say it again. Anticipation without expectation.

Thank You for Calling

The next suggestion is a deceptively simple one, yet a very powerful method for creating an opening through which the spirits can visit: cultivate an attitude of gratitude. This might sound more difficult than it is, especially if it feels right now as though there is nothing for which to be grateful.

This was probably the case for a mother who lost her son. After she read an article I had written about spirits ringing bells to say "hi," she shared her disappointment that her son hadn't announced his presence by using one of his favorite bells to make a sound.

I responded to this disappointed mother by writing: "Not *all* spirits will use bells. Your son may very well surprise you by saying 'hi' in another way. One of the ways we can help loved ones to get through is to thank them in advance for trying—because we know they are."

Five days later, this mother contacted me again to report that although none of her son's bells had rung, something else unusual happened. After thanking her son for trying to get through, she went to bed. About an hour later, she was startled from sleep by the sound of bells. One of her son's favorite hats, a hat with bells on it, had fallen to the floor. This made her very happy, even though she wasn't sure whether the incident had been a coincidence or her son making contact.

At this point I figured that her son would attempt to say "hello" in an even more profound way. Neither I, nor his mother, was disappointed again.

About ten days later, this grieving mother reported that she had dreamed about her son. It was such a real experience that she couldn't deny it or explain it away. When her son spoke during the dream, he convinced her that he had survived death. She awoke believing that there is life after death.

This experience, which rolled out over days, illustrates what I've been telling people for some time. Grief by nature creates alienation. Gratitude by nature creates connection.

Dream On

When the mother in the previous story mentioned the dream of her son, I had no doubt that it was a visitation and not just wishful thinking. The reason I think so is because she felt that it was real. This is one of the earmarks of dream visitations. Visits from spirits in dreams are more likely to contain elements of everyday living rather than disjointed images or strange locations. One mother reported to me that when she visited with her son in a dream, they were sitting in what looked like a frat house, with well-worn furniture and a coffee table marked with condensation rings. When a friend of mine came to me while I was sleeping, we sat at the kitchen table and drank tea together.

The most popular way for loved ones in spirit to visit is in dreams. It is easier for us to "meet" the spirits in dreams because the body is at rest, and our minds aren't busy with daily tasks. While we sleep, our consciousness naturally expands beyond the limitations of our bodies.

Not long ago, I was talking on the phone with a lady living in Malibu, California. Her darling son in spirit, Donny, wanted me to tell her that he was glad for the visit they had had the night before in her dreams. He let me know that she had been disappointed because he hadn't visited with her in that particular way for some time. He showed me a picture of a beautiful beach and said that in her dream, they had been walking together on that beach. Donny's mother confirmed that she had dreamt of her son right after he passed but then hadn't had a visit for two years. She was thrilled to have walked on the beach with him in her dreams the night before as they often did when he was physically living with her in Malibu.

At events I'm often asked, "How do I know that a dream is a visit and not just a dream?" I usually answer with another question, "What were the colors like?" Responses to this question usually include words like "intense, awesome, and indescribable, like nothing on earth." A blind man told me that when his mother visited him in a dream, she was "dressed in the colors of the rainbow." Dream visits are indeed bright and full of light. One mother told me, "I should have brought sunglasses."

It is important at this point to provide a bit of advice concerning dream visits. The same guidance offered earlier when talking about how to look for day-to-day signs from your loved ones in spirit, applies here too: *assume nothing and don't speculate.* The reason I mention this is because even though they are having dream visitations, many people become distressed when the beloved spirit doesn't act in an expected way during their visits. "My daughter was standing there, but she didn't say anything," one distraught mother told me. "We always talked when she was on earth. Do you think she's angry because I couldn't bear to cremate her body?" she asked.

"Of course not," I reassured her. "A dream visit is often just a way that a spirit says, 'Hi, I'm alive.'" Not every spirit speaks in dreams.

Another mother was panicked because her daughter's mouth was moving in her dream, but there was no sound. She was sure that her daughter was trying to get a message to her, and she was frantic about why she might have been unable to do so. "Your daughter is practicing," I told her. Just as singers and actors work on their voices, sometimes the spirits need to do the same thing. A year later, this mother had another dream visit from her daughter. "I'm okay, Mom," her daughter said.

Often during sessions, a spirit will mention that he or she is trying to come in dreams, but that the person they wish to visit isn't sleeping well. Following the death of someone we love, it isn't unusual for *all* life's routines, including sleep, to become completely disrupted. This can create a situation in which it is difficult to hear from those we love when we need it the most. During periods of grieving, it helps to get support from friends, support groups, and counselors. In actively working through grief, we're creating space for the spirits to have a place in our life.

I can't stress enough that the spirits are opportunists. They will use any means available to get through and may even work around the obstacles that grief can cause. Also, it is important to note that if your son, daughter, mother, father, sister, or brother is appearing in someone else's dream, don't worry. They are not avoiding you! They're just finding an open conduit elsewhere. When we become disconnected from life because of someone's death, we also become disconnected from the energy of the spirits. Grief can cause us to become either unplugged or plugged up (in terms of energy flow). In the appendix, "Is Anybody There?—How Everyone Can Become More Aware of Those in Spirit," I'll provide some exercises that can help those who are disconnected to plug in to life again and those who are plugged up to break through the blockages caused by grief.

Animal Instincts

Another way that the spirits let us know that they're around is by influencing animal behavior. Family pets are particularly susceptible to the presence of the spirits. While getting my hair cut the other day, my stylist mentioned that her dog was barking that morning at a dried wreath of roses from her grandmother's funeral. She was absolutely convinced that her dog was seeing her grandmother.

When a woman named Carol came for a session, her son in spirit said, "I'm playing with Toby." I assumed that Toby was his brother or a friend. Actually, Toby was his dog! Carol told me that since her son died, his dog grabs a toy and runs back and forth in front of her son's bedroom.

In my home, the cats are always on spirit alert. Sometimes it looks as though the three of them are watching a tennis match. Their fuzzy heads move back and forth in unison. I know that sometimes my cousin Tommy is running back and forth just for fun.

Winged creatures including birds, dragonflies, and butterflies are easily influenced by spirits as well. Bernie, a woman from northern California, asked me, "How can I know when my mother is around me? I can't have a medium with me all the time!" During our session together, her mother provided different signatures for each member of the family: Chanel No. 5 for her father, butterflies for her, and eagles for her son. After I mentioned each one, Bernie's eyes widened. "My mother's favorite perfume was Chanel No. 5, and my father gave it to her for every birthday. My mother gave me a butterfly dish, and before she died she told me that if butterflies were around, she would be too." Bernie mentioned that her son loves eagles and has an eagle sculpture on his desk. Bernie's mother personalized each of her signatures so that when they appeared, each one in her family would know that the "hello" was especially for them.

Bernie's mother then flashed a picture into my mind of a kid in a snowsuit. She reminded Bernie that she used to bundle her up before letting her play in the snow. "After I died, you were a kid again in a snowsuit," Bernie's mother said. "You were so bundled up in layers of grief you couldn't move forward or feel my touch. Take your snowsuit off, honey. It's sunny and warm."

One son in spirit told his mother, Jody, during a session that he was there with all the birds in her yard. "Oh yeah, that was really weird," she said. "One morning when I was feeling particularly sad, I looked off the deck and the yard was filled with birds. It scared me at first, but they started to fly up into the trees, onto the roof, and even onto the railing of the deck. Before I knew it, I was surrounded by birds."

I agree with Jody that the bird thing was out of the ordinary. However, unusual animal, bird, and bug behavior can be an indicator that the spirits are around. Every time a butterfly flutters by, it doesn't necessarily mean that someone in spirit is saying "hello." However, if you're standing in Antarctica and a butterfly alights on your finger, let's just say that either a spirit is present, or climate change is really escalating.

Technically Speaking . . .

Spirits like making noise because it gets our attention. On my Facebook page, a mother posted the following story about how her son in spirit lets her know that the beat goes on: "I keep a small conga drum next to the fireplace on the floor, and when I came home the other night I could swear that I heard someone tapping away on it while I sat on the couch. My son was a musician and a trickster! And I'm pretty sure that he's the one who is constantly knocking much louder around the house at night."

The spirits can have lots of fun with wind chimes, too. I love the sound of chimes, but I ultimately had to take mine down because they rang so much that the neighbors complained.

When a father in spirit promised his daughter that he would ring the wind chimes, he made good on his promise. Here's what she posted on my Facebook page: "At a session with you, my father came through and mentioned that he saw the work we were doing in our backyard and that we took the wind chimes down. In fact, my husband had taken them down and left them on the picnic table. You mentioned that my father said he would try to ring them even when there was no wind or when they weren't hanging. At times I would hear them chime in the middle of the night. One evening my husband (who was a huge skeptic at the time) ran in from the garage and said that the wind chimes were ringing loudly while he was in the garage. He turned to look at them and they were still on the table—no wind. Weeks later, while I was inside cooking dinner, my husband ran in again and stated that our son (who was two at the time) looked up at the wind chimes (which were hanging once again) and said, 'There's Grandpa.' So needless to say we call them 'Dad's wind chimes' and know we are getting a big hello from him every time they ring."

For my monthly newsletter, I wrote an article about how spirits like to use technology to say "hello." Readers responded with many stories of how loved ones in spirit are using cell phones, iPods, DVD players, computers, and almost anything else that has an electrical power source to communicate.

A mother whose son died three years ago was shocked to see her son's cell phone number displayed when her own cell rang one day. When she answered, no one was there (at least, in the physical sense).

Daniel, who had a similar experience, posted the following message on my Facebook page: "Recently I've been getting phone calls on my cell phone from a (555) 000–0000." He then went on to say that his garage door started opening and closing randomly on the day that his neighbor died. When the technician could find nothing wrong with the door's mechanism, Daniel thought that his neighbor must be saying "hello." The reason he thought so was not only because the activity started on the day of his neighbor's death, but because the door had fallen on his neighbor once by accident.

This brings me to another important point. Neighbors, relatives, and friends in spirit will often use the context and location of activity as another identifier. For instance, when the light in her car goes on and off, one mother has no doubt that her son, Luke, is saying "hello." Here's what she posted on my Facebook page: "Before my son died, he showed me how to turn off the tire light in my Mini Cooper. Since his death in 2005, that light comes on and turns off for no apparent reason. I know it's my son letting me know he's near."

Music is another way that loved ones in spirit let us know that they're near. A favorite song may start playing when the car radio is turned on, or, as happened to one mother, a daughter in spirit selected the music that played on her iPod.

When I had a session with Debra, Elton John's song "Don't Let the Sun Go Down on Me" started playing in my head. I mentioned this to her, and she understood immediately. Debra's daughter, who appeared to me as a real punk rocker decorated with lots of tattoos and piercings, didn't seem like the typical Elton John fan, so I was surprised that I kept hearing his music in my head. Debra explained why his music was so significant to her and her daughter.

Six months before she died at the age of twenty-three, Debra's daughter became obsessed with Elton John's ballads and played his music constantly. Debra, also a music lover, has an iPod packed with more than four thousand songs. One day when Debra was crying and saying to her daughter that she couldn't go on without her, she turned to the iPod for comfort. Although the iPod was on shuffle, one Elton John song played after another. Just when Debra thought that this was the result of the iPod going off shuffle, a Christmas song would play. Debra's daughter loved Christmas and Elton John. She loves her mother too. Debra is convinced that the iPod anomaly was her daughter's way of saying, "I'm with you."

Too Many Clues to Number!

Spirits can use numbers as signatures as well. A mother posted the following story on my Facebook page: "My son had a fascination with airplanes from the time he was very small. Ever since he passed, it seems as though I'm drawn to look at a clock when the time says 7:37 or 7:47. These were his favorite planes. He also saved pennies. When we need to know that he's with us, we always find a penny in the most unusual places or under the oddest circumstances."

I wish that I had a penny for every time I've heard a "pennies from heaven" story. Almost always, pennies from heaven look newly minted no matter how old they may be. These days, the spirits seem to be taking inflation into account because there are reports of quarters appearing out of nowhere as well.

Coins aren't the only gifts that the spirits give. A young woman named Carey told me that she had begun collecting all of the white feathers that were frequently appearing. She was convinced they were her mother's way of letting her know that she was around. "One day I noticed a white feather floating in a muddy puddle. When I picked it up, it was perfectly clean and white," she told me. "Mom's feathers are always clean and very white."

Sometimes loved ones in spirit can be creatively complex in their communications. As a medium, I've been complicit in several of their schemes without even knowing it. Here is one of my favorite examples of creative love in action.

During a small group event, a young mother named Darla recounted this story:

When I saw you about two years ago, my daughter came through and started talking to you about bumblebees. I had no idea what you were talking about. You insisted that my daughter was showing you little bumblebees. You also mentioned a birthday cake. My birthday had been two days before, so I accepted that my daughter was talking about my birthday. Although I didn't understand what the bumblebees meant, you told me to keep the information. My daughter was telling you that I would understand in the days ahead.

My daughter didn't let me down. The next day I struggled to go to work because it was the anniversary of her death. Coworkers at my new job didn't know about my grief. I had been very careful not to talk about it. They did, however, know about my birthday. A coworker (who loved to bake cakes) arrived that Monday morning with one of her creations. She brought it over to my desk on a covered cake plate. "I know that your birthday was Friday, but we'll just have to celebrate it today." With that, she uncovered the cake. To my astonishment, the cake was covered with candy bumblebees. I started to stutter out a thank you, to which she replied. "I was at a baking conference this weekend, saw these little bumblebees and couldn't resist putting them on the cake for you." After a bit more probing, I discovered that she had been buying the bumblebees at about the same time my daughter was talking to you about bumblebees and a birthday cake.

Darla's daughter definitely didn't let her down.

Photographic Memory

Spirits also like to pose for family photographs. One woman sent me an e-mail saying that when she took a Polaroid picture, the image of her father in spirit began to appear as the photo was developing. However, when the photograph was completely developed, all that remained was a streak of light where he had been standing.

Several years ago while I was dancing at a birthday celebration, friends took photos. In them, I was completely surrounded by what appeared to be bubbles. I had no doubt that the "bubbles," often referred to as "orbs," represented the presence of my mother in spirit. She loved a good party and knew a number of the people at the celebration.

Spirit photography is nothing new. In years past, I spent many pleasant hours studying spirit photographs reproduced in long out-of-print books. The spirits looked like old-fashioned daguerreotypes or in some cases, gauzy manifestations of fuzzy faces. In these early examples it was required that a medium be present because ectoplasm, a material exuded by mediums, was used by the spirits to create their faces and bodies. Some of these photographs have been authenticated; others were the result of fraud.

Orbs, on the other hand, show up in photos whether an official medium is in the room or not. They are bubblelike and may be clear, opaque, or color-washed. Some orbs seem to have a "man in the moon" appearance. When the images are enlarged, a face may become visible.

This was the case when a friend and I took a much closer look at the orbs that seemed to be coming from his antique armoire. He was trying to take photos of the armoire so that he could sell it on Craigslist. But every photograph he took was marred by bubbles and it was starting to annoy him. Upon further examination, there was indeed a face in the orbs. When these photos were looked at in succession, it appeared as if the face was trying to turn away from the camera. The action in the photos viewed this way played out like stop motion animation.

The man in the photo was dressed in a sailor uniform, and I had the strong sense after looking at the photos in this way that he was attached to the energy of an item being stored inside the cabinet. When I asked my friend about that possibility, he mentioned bringing back an antique bracelet from a recent trip to New York. The bracelet was stored in the cabinet. Perhaps the spirit was connected to that item. My friend and I felt inspired to communicate with this particular spirit. During a small spirit circle with friends, we did just that and our suspicions were confirmed.

For the most part, however, orbs that appear in photographs taken of family are loved ones in spirit. A friend of mine took a series of photographs while his mother was removing items from the car in which his sister had died. Orbs seemed to be bouncing off his mother's head and shoulders. He had no doubt that this was his sister's way of giving his mother a spirit hug.

Delightful orb photos were sent to me by the friend of a woman who had lost her son. After taking several photos in quick succession of a black puppy posing in a wing-back chair, she noticed an orb "posing" right next to him. In the next photo, the orb is gone. In the second photo, the puppy is blurred because it turned to look at where the orb had been. If I could draw a little thought balloon over the puppy's head, it would say, "Where'd ya go?" The woman, never having seen an orb before, thinks that her son in spirit was sitting right next to her new puppy.

Sometimes the spirits are moving so quickly that they appear as arcs of light streaking across a photograph. In one photo posted to my Facebook page, a young girl is surrounded by dancing swirls of light. This little girl informed everyone that she was dancing with her daddy, who had died not long before.

In other cases, a mist will appear in photos taken indoors where no smoke or fog was visible before the photo was taken. In one photograph sent to me by a client, a mistlike presence covers the face of her sister while she is sleeping. Previously, her sister had mentioned feeling something brush against her cheek at night. They decided to take the photograph as an experiment of sorts. They believe that the mist caught in the photo is their mother giving one of her daughters a goodnight kiss.

Sometimes spirits opt to say "hi" with existing pictures of themselves rather than appearing as orbs in photos. During a session, a teenager in spirit told his mother, "My face fills up your computer." I figured that this was because his mother was using a photo of her son as a screensaver. When I mentioned this to her, she said, "Oh no. I couldn't bear to look at photos of my son right after he passed. It was too painful for me. Then one day when I turned on my computer, his face was filling the screen. I yelled at everyone else in the family because I thought that they had done it. However, it kept happening and it wasn't always the same photo, but they were all photos of my son in happier days."

A young man in spirit was a master at sending photos of himself to his parents—by fax machine. In the early morning hours, the fax machine would start up by itself and then spit out a photo. This didn't happen just once or twice, but a number of times. When his parents relayed this story in front of the crowd at a group event, there were lots of "oohs" and "ahhs." This young man was tremendously personable and sociable; I enjoyed speaking with him. He threw information to me very quickly that I relayed to his parents just as quickly. "I went to my funeral before I died" popped out of my mouth. I stopped suddenly. "I'm so sorry," I said to the young man's parents. "I must have heard that incorrectly."

"Oh, you heard right," his mother said. "We had a memorial

service for our son the evening before we removed him from life support." After making such a heart-wrenching decision, it doesn't surprise me that her son is sending photos in such an extraordinary way.

Spirits may also superimpose their image onto another person. "You look just like my daughter," one mother said to me. Her daughter had died at the age of sixteen. I know that when someone says that I look like a sixteen-year-old girl, that the spirits have a hand in it. Sometimes when I'm working, the spirits get so close that they cover me with their energy and I take on their likeness. This also happens to me sometimes when I'm looking in the mirror, especially in the middle of the night. This used to be tremendously disconcerting, but now I take it in stride.

I am not the only one who the spirits can use to "appear" in the flesh. A number of my clients report seeing the one they love in a crowd, at the mall, or the grocery store. One mother decided not to chase these physical apparitions after startling more than one stranger with her advances. Now when she thinks that she sees her son, she says in her mind, "Hi, Ryan. Thanks for letting me know that you're around."

The spirits may also literally speak (or shout).

One mother told me that at around 4:00 a.m. she became fully awake when she heard, "Mom!" She got up out of bed, checked in to be sure that her children were sleeping safely and soundly. When she got back into bed she wondered if it was possible that Dugan, her son in spirit, was calling her. Dugan had died of a rare, undetected heart defect three years before. By the time she started her day later that morning, she had convinced herself that she had imagined the incident. However, for the following two mornings, she was awakened again at 4:00 a.m. by a voice calling out, "Mom!" After the third day she knew that it wasn't her imagination and she thanked her Dugan for shouting "Mom!" just like he used to do.

When doing an event in San Diego, California, I approached a lady sitting in the second or third row. Her hair was black, short, and curly. She was neatly, though casually, dressed and sat up very straight in her chair. As my attention became directed toward her, she drew back against the chair and seemed reluctant to participate. I couldn't ignore her, however, because a young man, a serious young man, was standing behind her. I mentioned this to her and she said, "No, I don't know a young man who has died. No." She was negatively definitive. Yet the young man wasn't moving.

"He's giving me the name Justin," I said, hoping that this would jog her memory.

"No, I don't know a Justin," she said.

I responded with "Well, I don't know what to tell you. Please remember that I mentioned Justin to you. You may realize who this is later on."

As I started to turn away I heard a voice shout "I'm here!" I turned back to the woman to ask, "Did you say something?" She was sitting even more upright in her chair, her eyes widened and startled. "Yes, I know Justin, but I don't want to talk to him."

This lady wasn't the only one startled. *Everyone* in the audience had heard Justin say "I'm here." He was a boy who would not be denied. As one lady in the group said later, "The real miracle was that we didn't all run for the door."

That's an important point, though. Even hearing a spirit

voice in the air (and outside of my head) didn't frighten people in the group. Justin just surprised them with his determination. I wish that I could tell you why Justin was being so insistent. I'm sure that all of us in the room that day were curious about his reasons for showing up and the lady's reasons for not wanting to speak with him. However, Justin didn't tell me why and neither did she. In situations like this I don't push the issue, knowing that sometimes a new way of relating often begins with a simple greeting enforced by great effort.

Kids in spirit are persistent when it comes to saying "hello" to those they love. Whether they visit in dreams, play with electronics, express themselves through music, or show up in a photograph, the simple message is, "I'm here." And sometimes, that is enough at first because it is an introduction to a new way of relating.

Spirit ANSWERS

What is the most effective thing to say to get a spirit to communicate with us? Does saying "please" work?

On earth, "please" may be the magic word, but when it comes to talking with the spirits, "thank you" is much more useful. Being grateful helps *us* to be more receptive to hearing from those we love in spirit. Before events or private sessions, I always thank the spirits for being there and for helping me do the work. I walk through my life knowing that I'm not alone. That certitude doesn't come from any confidence in my own capabilities and talents. It comes from the attitude of gratitude that I cultivate each and every day. Thank your loved ones in spirit for being around you, even if you're not sure that they're there. Try it and see what happens. Then let yourself be surprised.

If spirits can affect the physical world, will they remove obstacles from my path? Watch over me? Make things easier for me day to day?

The spirits will never do for us what we can and need to do for ourselves. Think of it this way. If a baby's mother never lets its feet touch the ground, the baby won't learn to walk. After a while its muscles will atrophy and the child will become crippled. The spirits don't carry us because the last thing they want is for us to become spiritual cripples. What they will do is inspire us with ways to remove the obstacles ourselves. They may also bring people into our lives to help us climb over the obstacles we come up against.

Yes, the spirits watch out for us, but that doesn't mean that there won't be challenges in life. Sitting around and asking the spirits to make life easier won't make life easier. That's because the one thing that the spirits can't overcome is our inertia. However, if you start moving, even if you're not sure where you're going, the spirits can guide you.

Is the bogeyman real? Are there restless souls caught between here and heaven? If so, how can we help set them free?

Fortunately, I've never met the bogeyman. I have, however, met some thoroughly unpleasant characters in spirit who choose to remain attached to earth's experiences. Because I work specifically with loved ones in spirit and guides, my everyday contact with troubled spirits is extremely limited. There are mediums who are dedicated to rescuing restless souls.

Doing this kind of work can be very demanding, however. It is not for the faint of heart.

Spirit SUMMARY

As a result of the increasing interest in spirit communication in recent years, many people are reporting their own interactions with loved ones in spirit. The spirits may say "hi" in different ways, but their message is often a very simple one: *we are here in love*. Spirits may visit in dreams, appear in pictures as orbs or streaks of light, and even leave "pennies from heaven" for you, but it is important not to restrict their expression by imposing expectations on the way *we* think they should appear to us. By cultivating an attitude of gratitude, especially for the blessings those in spirit have brought you over time, you're inviting them to make themselves known in your life again.

Is Anybody There?

How Everyone Can Become
More Aware of Those in Spirit

Spirit TWEET

"Shouting is hard from heaven, so listen for the whispering." (Said by a young man in spirit to his parents when they asked to hear from him.)

Spirit THOUGHTS

Sometimes when I'm beginning to "tune in," I hear what sounds like whispering in the background. It is almost like white noise. Whether you hear the whispers or not, those living in the spirit world are interacting with us. There is no need to worry about missing a message from someone you love in spirit. The message will get through some way, somehow. It is easy to think that mediums are the only ones relaying messages from the spirits, but that's just not true. Spirits may inspire a coworker or even a stranger to pass on a "hello."

A friend of mine was surprised one day when a colleague said to him, "How's it going, pumpkin?" He asked her why she called him "pumpkin" and immediately, she was embarrassed.

"I have no idea," she said. "It was out of my mouth before I knew it." My friend, who was having a difficult time, was comforted by the endearment. His grandmother had called him "pumpkin" and by the spontaneous greeting of his coworker he had no doubt that his grandmother was around.

My friend's colleague may not even consider herself psychic, much less a medium. Yet that didn't matter to his grandmother. The spirits know something about us that we ourselves may not be willing to accept. Being psychic is natural for all of us. Because it is an innate talent, it can be practiced, improved, and refined. Psychic ability can be expanded to include hearing from spirits. Even if you think that you're as dense as a door, hearing from the spirits is possible for you too. It really is.

The last thing that I want to do is create unrealistic expectations in situations where grief runs very deep, so please keep in mind that developing natural psychic talent is a process and for some people, this process takes years. However, what I can do in this chapter is provide some communication hints that, with practice, have the potential to help anyone become more aware of loved ones in spirit.

I'd also like to stress that hearing from the spirits may not be a consistent and regular occurrence. There may be weeks and even years between "hellos." Again, this is not an indication that someone you love has abandoned you. Just as there is a natural ebb and flow of energy in our lives, there is a natural rhythm to relationships as well—even those that continue beyond what we call death. The more aware we become of the energy of our lives, the more attuned we are to the rhythm of life on earth . . . and in the afterlife.

Because I think that living in this awareness is a natural yet forgotten way to be, I created a word to describe it. That word is "psy-conscious™." When we live "psy-consciously," the natural psychic part of ourselves informs our conscious thinking process. Instead of pitting the psychic part of ourselves against our logical minds, living psy-consciously is a melding of the two that results in a whole and complete approach to life. In essence, it is the way the spirits live. I've learned it from them, and I'd like to pass some of what I've learned along to you.

The exercises and meditations in this chapter provide opportunities to live psy-consciously and become more receptive to hearing from the spirits. Of course I can't cram everything I know into a few exercises, but with practice, these exercises will start you on a path to a way of living that includes those in spirit.

Walking Loud—How Listening to Your Foot-steps on Earth Can Connect You to Heaven

Go for a walk. Sounds simple, right? Well, this isn't just any way to walk.

Many people think that becoming more aware of the spirits means that we need to leave the body behind and go to where they are. Not so! It may feel counterintuitive, but the more you feel yourself in your body, the easier it is for the spirits to use your senses to get noticed. This exercise is an introduction to approaching life with more awareness. "Walking loud" is especially important for people who have recently suffered a great loss. It is a way to feel connected again to

your body, to others, and to the world, rather than feeling
separated from everything.

1. Put on comfortable shoes. If you are walking on the
    beach or on another surface that will not harm your
    feet, shoes aren't necessary.

2. Before starting your walk, stand with feet slightly
    apart, one foot in front of the other. Rock back and
    forth slightly until you can feel where your weight is
    the most centered. Rest for a moment in that cen-
    tered place.

3. Start walking naturally. As you take your first step,
    notice how your foot feels upon making contact
    with the ground.

4. As you continue walking, pay attention to how your
    feet feel. You can even imagine that your shoes have
    little magnets on the bottom that help attach your
    feet to the ground. If you're walking barefoot, pay
    attention to how the sand, the grass or the dirt feels.
    Is it cool underfoot? How do the grains of sand feel
    between your toes?

5. Listen to the sound of your feet as they connect to
    the ground. Notice the rhythm.

6. As the rhythm of your walking becomes more steady
    and established, begin to listen to the other sounds
    around you. Are birds singing? Are waves crashing
    or gently rolling to shore. Do you hear the voices of
    other people being carried on a breeze?

7. As you continue walking, turn your attention to the
    smells that surround you. Do you smell the scent of

flowers? The salt of the ocean? The aroma of food cooking at a nearby restaurant or home?

8. Continue walking. Attentive to all of the above—your feet on the ground, the rhythm of your steps, the sounds and smells around you.

9. At any time, if you feel overwhelmed by emotions, return your attention to the sound of your feet on the ground. Feel your feet connecting with the surface of the earth.

10. As you're walking, notice the colors around you. The blue of the sky, the green of the grass, the brown of the dirt under your feet. How many different types of blues are in the sky? What shades of green can be found in blades of grass? How does sun and shadow change the color of the path before you?

11. Continue walking, listening to the sounds that your feet make when they hit the ground. Pay attention to how your feet feel when they connect to the earth.

12. As you're walking, notice how the air around you tastes. Is it salty? Does it taste as though it is going to rain? Does it taste like spring? Or fall? Or winter?

13. Remember, if at any time you feel overwhelmed by emotions or experience sensory overload, just return your attention to your feet as they touch the ground. Listen to the rhythm of your walking. Walk loud.

If you have limited mobility, this exercise can be adapted to your situation. Even if you must remain in a chair, being outside on a natural surface would be helpful. If you are able to pick up your feet, then "walk" as you're sitting, following the steps within this exercise in the same manner, but from your seated position.

The Hamster Ball—How Building a Ball of Protection Can Help

When a neighbor came over to visit, she brought her hamster ... and his plastic ball. The ball was considerably larger than he was. When she brought him inside, he took off and ran around my place, rolling around inside the ball and oblivious to my three kitties. In fact, my cats took off, terrified by the rolling monstrosity, powered solely by the furry creature inside. This little guy was my inspiration for this exercise, which I call the Hamster Ball.

While growing in awareness to the spirits, it is important to be very well grounded, which the practice of Walking Loud can help accomplish. It is also important to create a protected space around your body that will allow your awareness to expand while setting a boundary that you control.

I've been practicing putting a ball of protection around myself for years. Being naturally sensitive, it has been helpful in shielding me from the frantic energy at airports and crowds. When I'm in my ball, I'm aware of what is going on around me yet I don't feel vulnerable.

The Hamster Ball exercise can be helpful for anyone who is feeling overly sensitive because of the loss of someone close. If going out in public is challenging, doing this exercise beforehand can help diffuse the intensity of the experience and put you back in control.

This exercise may be done sitting or standing, whichever feels more comfortable.

1. Feel your feet on the ground. Imagine that the bottoms of your feet are held in place by magnets or that your feet are sinking into the ground.

2. Once your feet feel comfortably anchored, imagine that a clear, translucent, white or gold ball is starting to grow out from underneath them. Although you can make your ball as large as you like, start small. Imagine that you can stretch out your arms in every direction and feel the wall of the ball.

3. The walls of the ball don't have to be hard or solid. They can have an elastic quality that will give as you move.

4. When building your ball, you can establish the boundaries of what is allowed and what isn't however you see fit. If you'd like to be open to being aware of your loved ones around you, then set that intention. If you want to allow good memories, set that intention. You are creating a ball of protected space; you can make it whatever you'd like.

5. In going about your day, check once in a while to be sure that your feet are comfortably anchored and your ball is still surrounding you.

Living in a ball has become second nature to me. Since some people say that my schedule makes me run around like a hamster in a ball, it is certainly appropriate. However, in this space that I've created for myself, life doesn't seem frenetic. As I set the intent for the day, life has a more directed aspect. Whenever I have to navigate through crowds at concerts, farmer's markets, and other events, I make a special effort to build the ball of protection around me.

Just as the hamster ball helped that little hamster who visited me face those big, scary cats, the Hamster Ball exercise can give you the confidence and security you need to keep from becoming overwhelmed when facing new challenges of your own.

An Attitude of Gratitude—A Simple Exercise for Thanking Those You Love

People often ask me for simple ways to feel closer to loved ones in spirit. I've discovered that one of the fastest and easiest is cultivating an appreciation for all the good things they brought into your life. When someone we love passes, it seems as though their place in our lives is also gone. But time and time again during sessions, the spirits come through and say things like, "Remember the time when . . ." The spirits emphasize good memories as a way to reclaim a relationship that seems to have been lost.

Another reason to be grateful for good times is that spirits often say "hello" in ways that will relate to them. Remember the mother whose daughter started playing Elton John songs on her iPod? If her sense of loss had driven her to put away all music because it reminded her of her daughter, that avenue of communication would have been closed off.

By expressing gratitude, the possibilities for communication are expanded, not contracted. As gratitude increases, so too are the ways that loved ones let you know they're around.

Here's what you'll need:

- A basket or box with a lid. (This can be as simple or as fancy as you'd like to make it.) You can cover the box with stickers, or draw pictures on it, or glue family photos to it.
- Individual pieces of paper. (Try using paper in the favorite color of your loved one, or in your own favorite color. Or choose the colors of the rainbow as that also establishes an energy conducive to a connection.)
- Pens, pencils, or markers.
- Photos and/or mementos of your loved ones (optional).

1. Say the name of the one you love aloud while looking at a picture of that person or while envisioning that person in your mind.

2. On individual pieces of paper, write down ways in which your life was enriched by that person's presence: i.e., a shared love of music, bad jokes that still make you laugh, encouragement that helped get you through school, fun you had together on family vacations, a kiss goodnight. Jot down as many as you can in five minutes. (You can always add more "gifts" later.)

3. You may also want to include the memories that others have shared about the one you love. These days, it is not uncommon for kids to post their thoughts on Facebook when a friend dies.

4. Thank your loved one for all the gifts he or she gave to you and gave to everyone else whose lives he or she touched.

5. "Gifts" can be selected from or added to the box at any time.

Maintaining an attitude of gratitude can help reclaim many wonderful blessings that we thought were taken by death. Whenever you're missing the one you love, open the box, pull out a "gift," and thank him or her for it. I assure you, your "thank you" will be heard by your loved one in spirit.

The Stage—Allowing Loved Ones in Spirit to Be Themselves

At mediumship development workshops, I stress the importance of allowing the spirits to present themselves *in their own way*. By setting expectations aside, we avoid creating hurdles for our spirit loved ones to jump over on their way to see us, and we effectively free up energy for them to communicate in whatever way they can. The fewer demands we place on the spirits to meet us on our own terms, the easier it is for them to meet us.

1. In order to use this exercise most effectively, I suggest you record it and then follow the steps by playing back the recording. This way you can create your own guided meditation.
2. Sit in an upright, straight-backed chair with your feet on the floor and your hands resting comfortably in your lap.
3. Close your eyes. Take several measured, deep breaths.
4. Imagine yourself sitting alone in a darkened theater. The aisles are lined with tiny white lights leading toward the stage before you.
5. In your mind, see yourself getting up from your seat in the theater and walking toward the stage.

6. When you reach the base of the stage, you notice stairs leading to it from the house floor.

7. As your foot rests on the first step, you notice that it begins to glow with the color red. As you stand with both feet on the red glowing stair, notice how the color feels. Do your feet feel warm while standing on the red stair? Cool? What emotions pass through you? Notice how you feel and then allow the feelings to pass through you.

8. Step onto the next stair. As your foot touches the tread, it begins to glow with the color orange. As you stand with both feet, notice how the color orange feels. What does the color orange taste like? And smell like?

9. Once you've spent a little time with the color orange, take the next step, landing on a tread that glows with the color yellow. As you pause on this stair, allow the color yellow to glow more brightly. Imagine you are surrounded by its light. Notice if you smell anything as you're bathed in yellow. What memories does the color bring to mind? Just allow images to float into your mind. Listen to the sounds that accompany the memories.

10. The next step glows green. As you stand on this color, allow yourself to be filled with its light. Where there is dis-ease or distress, allow the green to wash away pain and discomfort, touching your heart with healing. If you experience a sudden surge of grief, allow yourself to feel it and then let the color green fill your heart.

11. As you set your foot on the next riser, imagine that it glows with blue light. Allow the blue light to rise up around you and to swirl in your throat area. One of your ears might feel pressure, almost as though you're rising in altitude quickly.

12. The next step begins to glow with a rich indigo color. This particular color is the hue often seen on the horizon as the sun dips down at the end of a day. As you step into indigo, you may notice that it forms a horizon of sorts between the stairs and the stage.

13. The stage begins to glow with a deep violet light. As you step onto the stage, the light fills up the stage. The violet color becomes brighter and lighter until the entire stage begins to glow with a soft white light.

14. As your eyes become adjusted, you can see the stage filling up with those you love in spirit. Just observe how they look and see what they're doing. They may or may not acknowledge you at first. Just allow the scene to unfold as it will.

     Whenever I've used this guided meditation in a group, people have often been surprised by the results. One father saw his daughter in spirit surrounded by other family members in spirit. A mother saw her son in spirit playing hockey. She stood on the sidelines and cheered him on. A young woman saw her mother in a beautiful garden. Her mother gathered a bouquet together and gave it to her daughter as a gift.

15. After a few minutes, the white light begins to fade and the stage is filled with violet. As you turn to

walk back down the stairs, the treads below you begin to glow again. As you step onto each one, indigo, blue, green, yellow, orange, and red, in that order, the house lights begin to rise and the seats in the auditorium come into view.

16. In your mind, envision yourself walking to one of the auditorium seats and sitting down.

17. After a minute or two, become aware of what is going on around you. Listen to the noises in the house, notice smells wafting through the air. Wiggle your toes and your fingers. Feel your feet on the floor.

18. Once you're fully aware of your surroundings open your eyes.

19. Thank your loved ones in spirit for being with you and reflect on your experience.

I don't suggest that this guided meditation be done more than once every three months. People who have attended my workshop have reported that as a result of doing this meditation, they've become more aware of their loved ones saying "hi" in common everyday ways.

Whether we realize it or not, or are even willing to accept it as true, communication between humans and spirits is constant. This connection may be expressed when a musician wakes up with a new song in his head, or a loved one's photo falls off the mantel. We, as people, are finally beginning to understand what the spirits already know. We're not independent, we're interdependent.

Just imagine what it would be like sitting down at a big banquet table with your family and friends both living and dead.

At this table you are able to tell everyone exactly how their actions have impacted your life. They, in turn, can do the same. You might be surprised at what you hear! Maybe a nephew will thank you for helping put him through college. Or an uncle will remind you of how you used to laugh at his jokes. Or a daughter may say that criticism of her clothing caused her to give up her aspirations to be a fashion designer. Or a father may ask your forgiveness for drinking himself to death. Or a son may apologize for taking his own life.

We don't have to wait until we die ourselves to have this banquet experience. Those in spirit have enthusiastically answered the call to the table. They want to share in our lives here and now. Mediums are simply the placeholders for spirit at these family gatherings.

As a medium, I am humbled by the knowledge that I do this work only because those in spirit have called me to serve them. I stand in the gap that death has caused between those living on both sides of it. That gap, however, is narrowing as the years go by. More and more people are having their own personal encounters with spirits. I couldn't be more delighted at the possibility that one day we will all be so interconnected that there will be no need for mediums.

Until that day, I will be a placeholder for the spirits at the banquet table of life.

Invitation to the Banquet Table—Starting the Conversation with Loved Ones in Spirit

So how do we start communicating with loved ones in spirit? All communication starts by invitation. Whether preparing to meet with a medium, or exploring the possibility of experiencing a connection yourself, here's an exercise that can help. It's called "Invitation to the Banquet Table" and uses a technique called "visualization." Visualization is a fancy term for what we used to call imagination when we were kids.

This exercise is for beginners and those who are experienced in communicating with spirits. Before you begin the exercise, read it through from start to finish. This way you won't be interrupting yourself as you go along. If you'd like, you can also record the steps and play them aloud as you practice for the first time.

1. Sit in a comfortable, straight-backed chair with your feet flat on the floor and hands in your lap, palms facing upward, eyes closed.

2. As you sit, allow the chair to hold all of your weight. If you feel tension in any part of your body, take a breath and imagine that as you breathe out, the tension releases too.

3. In this relaxed state, you're still aware of sitting in a chair with your feet firmly on the floor. Sit quietly for a moment. If any stray thoughts enter your mind, just let them pass right on through.

4. Once your mind starts to quiet down, imagine a lovely pink light surrounding you and filling the entire room. Observe how this feels. This pink light creates a safe and loving space for you and your loved ones to meet.

5. In your mind's eye, imagine that you're sitting at a table. Let your imagination create the table for you. It can be as simple or elaborate as you'd like with as

many or as few chairs as you'd like. The table can be set with your heirloom china or paper plates if you'd enjoy a picnic instead. If you prefer mugs to crystal, that's fine, too. This is your table; create it exactly as you'd like.

6. As you gaze at the table, consider who you would like to invite to the banquet. You may even add a name card to a place setting, if you'd like.

7. Now that the table is ready, it is time to welcome your guest(s).

8. When you're ready, in your mind imagine a door to your left. The door is either violet or outlined in violet.

9. As the door opens, you may say in your mind, "Welcome _____." (Insert the name of your loved one in the blank space.)

10. First, observe how your loved one looks. Don't be surprised if they seem younger or healthier than you remember them. Allow them to be as they appear, and release any preconceived notions of how they should look to you.

11. If you'd like, feel free to say in your mind (or out loud) *anything* that you want to say. This can be as simple as "I love you," or a number of other things that have been pent up for some time. Let it all out—even if you're angry with them for dying. That's okay. You won't scare them away. Know that your loved one(s) can hear you even if they don't seem to respond.

12. When you are finished, sit silently for a few moments. Notice any thoughts that might pop into your mind.

It is easy to discount these thoughts as your own, but don't dismiss them too easily. Memories may suddenly come to the surface. Often our loved ones want to remind us of the good times.

13. Thank your loved one(s) for responding to your invitation. Allow them to leave the table and depart through the violet doorway.

14. Glance at the table once again. Sometimes those we love will leave something on it as a gift. Maybe it is a rose. Maybe it is a toy. Maybe it is a card.

15. Accept the gift that may be left behind with thanks.

16. Once again feel yourself in your chair, feet on the floor, hands in your lap. Allow yourself to become aware of what is going on around you in the room.

17. When you're ready, open your eyes.

Each time you use "Invitation to a Banquet," those who are welcomed may be different, and the experience may be different. It is an opportunity to begin and continue to meet with your loved ones living in spirit.

The Patchwork Quilt—Putting Together the Pieces of Spirit Communication

One of the best ways I've found to help people recognize the difference between their own wishful thinking and actual communications from spirit, is to create what I call the Patchwork Quilt. With diligent use of this exercise, the sum of minor incidents of spirit communication can reveal a deeper, more significant pattern.

As I've described in this book, sometimes the spirits give me information in bits and pieces—a name here, a feeling there, a picture in my mind or a symbol. Sometimes missing pieces of a communication will show up for clients days, weeks, or even years after the initial contact, creating even greater understanding.

The Patchwork Quilt exercise is a way for you to assemble bits and pieces of spirit communication so that you can start to see the entire quilt. During our daily routines, there might be little things that happen here and there that make you think, "Could that be the one I love saying 'hello'?" It is easy to dismiss these little incidents as coincidence or figments of the imagination. However, by making a record of what happens and when, patterns begin to emerge.

Keep a small pad with you to jot down anything that seems as though it could be a greeting from the spirits. Don't worry about whether it seems significant or not. It could be as simple as seeing a license plate with your loved one's name on it.

The examples in chapter 10 will help you to make an outline of the way that a greeting may come. If you have a dream of someone in spirit, write it down. If you smell a familiar aftershave when there is no one around, write it down. If an orb appears in a photo, write it down. Write everything down including where and when the events occurred.

Don't be alarmed if time goes by and it seems as though nothing is happening. Sometimes activity increases around holidays and family activities.

If your friends and family members keep logs of their own, you may be surprised at the patterns that can emerge when you compare notes.

The important thing to remember is that your loved ones in

spirit are trying to reach you. With an open mind, an open heart, and an attitude of gratitude, you'll be ready to hear from them.

Ten Things That Make Talking to Kids in Spirit Unique

1. Kids are superenthusiastic.
2. Kids have no consciousness of death—even those who have suffered with long illnesses. (They're right that we don't die. Death is just not a major part of their life.)
3. Kids like to talk to other kids, even if they're not related to them.
4. Kids are persistent—sometimes extremely so.
5. Kids are playful with communication. They like to affect the physical world.
6. Kids challenge all assumptions about life and death.
7. Kids are curious—even as spirits, they like to test boundaries.
8. You can't make kids do anything or answer any question they don't want to.
9. Kids are always learning.
10. Kids tell it like it is! Always.

What We Can Learn From Kids in Spirit

- Play always, but don't always play by the rules.
- Bullies might win on the playground, but they lose at the game of life.
- Life is like skateboarding. You'll fall a lot before mastering the tricks.

- Live at the speed of light. Laugh at the speed of sound.
- "Why?" is a short question that takes eternity to answer.
- Life is like playing on the swings. It's more fun the higher you go.
- Don't wait until school's out to enjoy life.
- Let your life tell a story that inspires.
- Don't grow up, just keep growing.
- Live beyond limits because life is limitless.
- Share your toys and you'll always have joy.
- If you think that you're singing alone, just listen. There's always a band playing behind you.
- Don't be afraid of the bogeyman under the bed. He can't keep you from dreaming.
- Saying "thank you" rather than "please" is the way to receive what you need.
- Sometimes a butterfly is a kiss from heaven.
- Forgiveness changes life from black-and-white to color.
- Death is life changing, but it is better to change before dying.
- The building blocks of heaven are love, hope, and joy.

The Spirits' Declaration of Interdependence

We hold these truths to be self-evident:

1. That we remain interested in the details of your life: noticing the new dress you bought for a special occasion, the "to do" list that needs to get done, the leak under the kitchen sink, the hobbies that we enjoy with you.

2. That we notice what you do for us in love: carrying a photo, lighting a candle, creating a charity, sharing stories with friends. (And we'll even allow you to exaggerate a bit.)

3. That we hear you when you talk to us before going to bed and in the car while driving to work. We answer sometimes through a song on the radio or the inspired words of a stranger.

4. That we want you to laugh, knowing that your returning joy is a celebration of our lives and grief needn't be the only expression of your love.

5. That when we come to you in dreams, it is a real visit and not your imagination.

6. That by healing the diseases of addiction, the betrayal of abuse in your own lives, and forgiving us for failing you and ourselves, wholeness touches us here and changes the path of those who come after you.

7. That although we won't interfere with your free will or that of others, we can help guide your decisions—and work from this side to bring harmony instead of discord. (We can't rewrite wills yet from the other side, so don't ask for that one.)

8. That we will be there for the holidays, the birthdays, the family reunions. We will walk you down the aisle at your wedding and share the joy when a baby joins the family. We especially like smiling at the babies who smile back.

9. That your love and thoughts don't keep us from moving on, but give us wings to fly to the farthest

reaches of heaven while still keeping us close to you. We can be in two places at once, you know.

10. That no matter how we passed, even if we ended physical life by our own hand, we will be waiting in heaven for you. And, yes, we will be together again . . . someday.

ACKNOWLEDGMENTS

Francis H. Gierisch—Dad, thank you for always believing in me.

Wendy, Bruce, Frankie, and Tyler—Thank you for being my family, a family that I love . . . and like.

Hope Innelli—Thank you for being equal parts editor and cheerleader. Your expertise, gentle coaxing, and sensitivity to the subject matter were appreciated more than I can say. (Please don't edit your own acknowledgment, just take the compliment!)

Jennifer Pooley—Thank you for enthusiastically grabbing a list of ideas from my hand at the SDSU Writers Conference and subsequently introducing me to the wonderful team that made this book happen.

Robert Brown—Thank you for showing me how the English mediums do it. Thank you for your unflagging dedication to spirit communication and for bringing me along on so many "spirited" journeys.

Kevin—Thank you for being my friend and doorkeeper.

John Edward—Thank you for your timely advice and for encouraging me to take leaps of faith.

Tom—Thank you for awakening the explorer in me.

Michelle—Thank you for walking beside me in my journey.

Ken—Thank you for sharing my darkest days and brightest nights.

Suzy—Thank you for pushing me beyond my limits.

Mary Anne—Thank you for sharing your life, your home, and your full refrigerator.

Angela—Thank you for your unfailing sense of direction.

Vanora—Thank you for being my soul friend.

Ashley—Thank you for taking care of the details.

Clay—Thank you for always being there.

Wendy—Thank you for appreciating my work before it was noticed by others.

Chi, Isis, Vandal, Rhaevan, and Koa—Thank you for your companionship and for keeping me laughing.

To all the mediums that have gone before—Thank you for serving the spirits, often at great personal cost. It is because of your work that mine has a place in the world.